Jangle jangle! Jewellery jewellery!

Now then, now then, now then! Goodness gracious – ladies and gentlemen, guys and gals! How are you all, how is the fabric of your person? As it 'appens, guys and gals, we will ask you to cast your minds back to the tremendous, the highly successful, the one and only *Never-Mind-the-Buzzcocks*, like thissss! Uhuhuhuh!

We will play a little more of the sig tune, you see, we will talk to Dignified Don and we will light up a stogie and introduce the fine trio of gentlemen who make it all possible, you see! Stand up straight!

Here to make some more dreams come true is my friend Uncle Hughes the Sean – the very marvellous comic Irish gentleman with the oh-so-lovely and hugely selling novels. Providing a most worthy opponent – although not in the pugilistic sense, for my friends are not imbibing in the acts of violence, you see – is the one and only Young Doctor Jupitus, the erstwhile Porky of the Poetic variety, goodness gracious. Finally – now then, now then, goodness gracious – last but by no means the least, the throwback of forty years ago, keeping a bequiff-ed eye on proceedings, Mr Mark of Lamarr – may the good Lord rest his soul!

I will give you one point for the artist, two points for the title! Open brackets, close brackets! Is that not right, Uncle Ted? Clunk click every trip, you seee! Stoke Mandeville, goodness gracious! We are not 'ere, we are running the marathon with all the lovely young ladies! Uhuh! The Duchess – God bless her!!! This is the age of the traaaain! When I press this button – tea-riffic! The lovely coldness of the young flesh, you see ...

Never Mind the Buzzcocks

A foreword by Jimmy Savile*

GREAT MOMENTS IN ROCK HISTORY

THE SEX PISTOLS SIGN FOR A&M (1977)

LIVE AID (1985)

CONNECTIONS

THE HOUSEMARTINS AND NEW KIDS ON THE BLOCK

'Connections' is the round that links pop music's unlikeliest bedfellows. Can you find a connection between loveable, playful and extremely left-wing eighties pop cynics, The Housemartins, and those terrifying thugs of New York's urban wastelands, New Kids on the Block?

PHILL   Are they both from Hull? You know, The Housemartins, fourth best band in Hull – New Kids on the Block, fifth best band in Hull? They used to be known as New Kids on the Docks.

MARK   I don't think the New Kids would rate that high even in Hull terms …

SHAGGY   The new Kids are from New Jersey – and The Housemartins all need new jerseys?

PHILL   The New Kids were known as NKOTB, which is an anagram of 't'knob', right? Which is what they were known as in Hull.

SUGGS   A Housemartin is a bird, which is how they got their name. And New Kids on the Block are a bunch of tits.

PHILL   Hughie of The Housemartins went to prison, and one of the New Kids attacked someone? Is that the link?

ANSWER:
The connection is that both bands have had members arrested for arson. In 1993, Housemartin Hugh Whitaker was jailed for six years after attempting to torch his ex-girlfriend's house. Two years earlier, Donnie Wahlberg of the New Kids was charged with first-degree arson after he set fire to the carpet in a Kentucky hotel room.

The damage from the hotel fire allegedly cost Donnie 2 million dollars. It would have cost 500 bucks but he doused the flames with the contents of the mini bar.

The Housemartins' drummer Hugh Whitaker was sent to jail for setting fire to a car dealer's house, using fireworks. Police caught him when he came back later to put foil-wrapped potatoes in the embers.

Chris Evans' Breakfast Show
Running Order 18 June

08.40 am: CHRIS:And don't forget it's British sitcom day on the show this morning.
(CHRIS TO HUM THEME TUNE OF 'TERRY AND JUNE')

CHRIS:Ronnie Hazelhurst, we're not worthy!
(CHRIS' ENTOURAGE TO CHEER IN AGREEMENT)

8.45 am: (CHRIS TO PLAY LATEST TEXAS SINGLE)

8.48 am: (CHRIS TO HUMILIATE ONE OF HIS ENTOURAGE FOR WEARING CORDUROY TROUSERS)

8.55 am: (CHRIS PLAYS PREVIOUS TEXAS SINGLE)

8.58 am (CHRIS TO PERSUADE LISTENERS TO THROW AWAY THEIR CORDUROY TROUSERS)

9.00 am (NEWS AND TRAFFIC)

9.01 am: (CHRIS TO HUMILIATE TRAINEE TRAFFIC-REPORT GIRL)

9.05 am: CHRIS:And don't forget it's British sitcom day on the show today

(CHRIS TO HUM THEME TUNE OF 'ONLY FOOLS AND HORSES)
CHRIS:John Sullivan, we're not worthy!
(ENTOURAGE TO CHEER IN AGREEMENT)

9.10 am: (CHRIS FIRES CORDUROY-WEARING MEMBER OF ENTOURAGE)

9.15 am: (CHRIS TO NAMEDROP GAZZA, NATALIE IMBRUGLIA, SHARLEEN FROM TEXAS AND DANNY BAKER, AND PRETEND HE'S INTERESTED IN FOOTBALL)

9.20 am: (ENTOURAGE CHEER AT THIS REMARK AND CHRIS' ACCOUNTANT TO SEND ROYALTY CHEQUE TO DANNY BAKER)

9.23 am: (CHRIS TO CASUALLY LET DROP HOW MUCH MONEY HE EARNED LAST YEAR)

9.25 am: (CHRIS TO PLAY OLD SIMPLY RED RECORD)

9.28 am: (CHRIS ASKS ENTOURAGE WHETHER HE'D LOOK GOOD WITH A MICK HUCKNALL HAIRSTYLE)

9.30 am: (CHRIS ASKS LISTENERS TO SEND IN DRAWINGS OF HIM WITH MICK HUCKNALL HAIRSTYLE. WINNER TO BE ALLOWED TO JOIN CHRIS' ENTOURAGE AND LAUGH UPROARIOUSLY AT HIS JOKES FOR THE DAY)

9.32 am: (CHRIS TO DELAY NEWS REPORT BY TELLING EXTENDED ANECDOTE ABOUT DRINKING IN FASHIONABLE WEST END BAR WITH MICK HUCKNALL, GAZZA, DANNY BAKER AND SHARLEEN FROM TEXAS)

WORD UP

THE HISTORY OF POP LYRIC WRITING HAS GIVEN US A GLOSSARY OF BIZARRE NEW WORDS AND PHRASES. 'WORD UP' IS ABOUT THE MEANINGS OF OBSCURE LYRICS EVERYWHERE.

'BISMILLAH' from BOHEMIAN RHAPSODY by QUEEN

In 1975 and 1991, Queen topped the chart for a total of fourteen weeks with that little-known b-side *'BOHEMIAN RHAPSODY'*, from which this line is taken:

'Easy come! Easy go! Will you let me go?
Bismillah! Nooo! We will not let you go!'

But what did Freddie and friends mean by *'BISMILLAH'*?

PHILL   Is it a word to describe four men in a darkened room, trying to blow out a very high candle?

SHOVELL   I think the actual pronunciation is a 'bi-smeller' – someone who sniffs the arses of men or women.

MARK   This isn't Call My Bluff, the pronunciation is 'bismillah'.

RICK WITTER   It's four in the morning … it's your last drink in the fridge … and you just don't care any more.

PHILL   Yeah, I'll have a bottle of Bismillah. Or Bismillah Light, perhaps? Or is it a word to describe the feeling you get when you wake up next to Anita Dobson?

MARK   Easy come, easy go.

RICK WITTER   Bismillah. Is that Windy Miller's sister?

PHILL   Is it a route to get to North Wales, taking in the B15, the M1 and finally ending up in the village of Llah?

SHOVELL   I went to school with a guy called Graham Breen, who was a massive Queen fan, so I know the answer. It's 'for the love of God', or something like that.

ANSWER:
You're basically there. 'Bismillah' is Arabic for 'in the name of God'. The ANC adopted Queen's 'I Want to Break Free' as an anthem symbolising their struggle against injustice and oppression. It was a toss-up between that and 'Fat Bottomed Girls' …

CONNECTIONS

CYNDI LAUPER AND JIMMY SAVILE

Can you find the link between quirky, rainbow-haired American songstress Cyndi Lauper, and 'Now then, now then, goodness gracious – uhuhuhuhuh! – the one and only Sir Jimmy Savile OBE, you seeee!'

MARK   Her face does imply that Jimmy Savile's in the room somewhere, doesn't it? She does look a bit …

PHILL   She does, yeah.

FRANK SKINNER
I think he's a goer, though, he's very fit is Jimmy. I bet he could go for hours. I bet if you have sex with Jimmy Savile, then afterwards you get a Mars Bar and a Bacofoil cloak.

LEEROY THORNHILL
I think there's some porn going on there. All that jewellery. He's caked in gold. There's got to be porn involved – it's far too expensive to have all that on.

MARK   So you think that the richest people in the world are those that star in porn films?

PHILL   You couldn't have Jimmy Savile in a porn film, you'd never be able to concentrate. 'Uhuhuh, you're a lovely lady, and I'm a plumber. I've come to fix your sink, love. Howzabout me repairing your plumbing?'

MARK   'Now then, now then, now then, what's that then?'

PHILL   Then, when he's actually having sex: 'Eh, oh, oh, oh, uh, oh, uhuh. Uhuhuhuhuh!'

FRANK SKINNER
The orgasm!

LEEROY THORNHILL
'Uhuhuhuh!'

MARK   I'm guessing that there might be other areas we could explore.

FRANK SKINNER

Well, if it had been Gloria Estefan instead of Cyndi Lauper, we could have done a 'clunk click, every trip' joke.

(AUDIENCE GROANS)

Ah, come on! Apparently her last two albums sold so well that her spine went platinum. Is it true that Jimmy Savile's hairdresser was so famous that they wrote an opera about him? That's this week's viewer's question – what would that opera be called? The prize is my dressing room key at the BBC. Any offers?

AUDIENCE MEMBER

The Barber of Savile.

FRANK SKINNER

Well done!
This is tragic, but I think I know. Jimmy Savile was a wrestler, big time. When I was a kid, in fact …

MARK

Really? You saw him?

FRANK SKINNER

Yeah, at the Hen & Chickens in Oldbury. It was 'Grab-a-Granny' night on Thursdays. Not attractive women, but lovely breakfasts. Anyway, Jimmy was a wrestler, and Cyndi Lauper worked in wrestling: she was a promoter or something like that.

ANSWER:
The unlikely answer is that both have connections with the world of wrestling. Sir Jimmy was a grappler in his younger days, while Cyndi was a WWF wrestling promoter during a lull in her career.
When Jimmy Savile was entertainments officer at Broadmoor Hospital for the Criminally Insane, he once booked a magician who sawed a woman in half. It was the only time that no-one in the audience had to ask how it was done.

The Many Faces Of David Bowie

Rock chameleon David Bowie is famous for his many bewildering changes of style and colour, his bulging eyes and his diet of aphids. Let's look now at the many phases of the Man Who Sold The World (not the Lulu version).

1. ALADDIN SANE 1973–75.
In the early 70s Bowie called into question the sexual ambiguity and psychological uncertainty of the 20th century by painting a blue stripe down his face.

2. CHARLIE CHAPLIN 1975.
Inspired by a Homepride packet, this retro look failed to take off, although the bowler hat and funny walk were very popular in Northern Ireland. Band members Trevor Bradford and Dave Bingley left to form a building society.

3. MRS PANKHURST AUG. 18 1975.
An even more short-lived phase which spawned the single 'Suffragette City'. Abandoned when it was pointed out to Bowie that he already had the vote, but not before he had hurled himself under Freddie Mercury.

4. PENELOPE KEITH 1975–77.
Bowie's chameleon-like skills were never more evident than in his Penelope Keith period. Such was his mastery of disguise that he actually spent four series as Margo. Spawned the single 'Good Life On Mars'.

5. THE BERLIN PERIOD 1977–80.
This bleak phase in Bowie's creative existence produced some of his most memorable music, but he also sometimes misjudged the public mood, as when he gave a Nazi salute at Waterloo station, rounded up gypsies and bombed Tilbury docks.

6. THE SKEGNESS PERIOD 1980–85.
The Eighties found Bowie in an even more bleak, windswept phase, so stark and moribund that the material was never actually released.

7. THOMPSON'S GAZELLE 1985–88.
After experimenting with hartebeest and eland looks, Bowie settled on this Thompson's gazelle image in the mid-1980s. Not one of his more successful periods, it came to an end when the bassist was eaten by a lion, making for disturbing Bank Holiday viewing.

**8. LEANING TOWER OF PISA.
2–2.30pm, 12 February 1987.**
A short-lived idea, which Bowie abandoned when he was declared structurally unsound.

9. TIN MACHINE 1987–89.
The wilderness years. Music so far ahead of its time it still hasn't happened yet.

10. GOING TO THE NEWSAGENTS IN SLIPPERS 1990.
Not actually an image this; Bowie was genuinely going to buy 20 Rothmans and a Pukka Pie. This didn't prevent thousands of fans feverishly following suit.

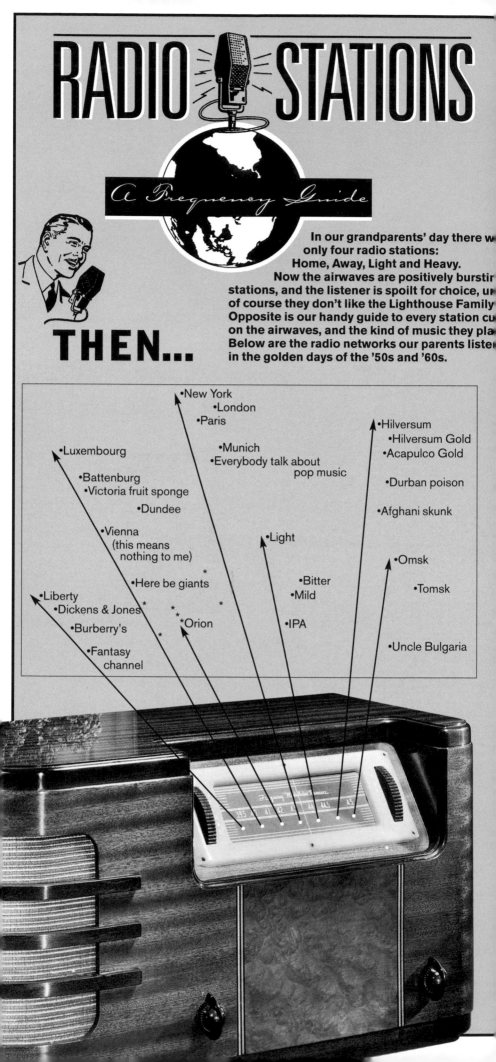

RADIO STATIONS

A Frequency Guide

In our grandparents' day there w
only four radio stations:
Home, Away, Light and Heavy.
Now the airwaves are positively burstir
stations, and the listener is spoilt for choice, u
of course they don't like the Lighthouse Family
Opposite is our handy guide to every station cu
on the airwaves, and the kind of music they pla
Below are the radio networks our parents liste
in the golden days of the '50s and '60s.

THEN...

•New York
•London
•Paris
•Munich
•Everybody talk about
  pop music

•Hilversum
•Hilversum Gold
•Acapulco Gold

•Durban poison

•Afghani skunk

•Luxembourg

•Battenburg
•Victoria fruit sponge
•Dundee

•Light

•Vienna
(this means
nothing to me)

•Omsk

•Tomsk

•Here be giants *

•Bitter
•Mild

•Liberty
•Dickens & Jones *
•Burberry's   * *
•Fantasy   *Orion
channel

•IPA

•Uncle Bulgaria

NOW...

RADIO STATION	MUSIC POLICY
Love Over Gold	All the hits of Dire Straits
Dire FM	All the other hits of Dire Straits
Capital Gold	All the hits of Dire Straits
Capital Gold Gold	All the old hits of Dire Straits
H.A.P.P.Y. Radio	24-hour jollity
U.N.H.A.P.P.Y. Radio	24-hour jollity from the United Nations
Hoddesdon & Broxbourne General Hospital Radio (Alderman Arthur W.Tunicliffe Ward)	Dire Straits and traffic, weather and hourly reports on Mr Cullen's peptic ulcer
Hoddesdon & Broxbourne General Hospital Radio (Alderman Arthur W.Tunicliffe Ward Gold)	Dire Straits and Classic Illnesses
Rant FM	Controversial talk radio
Controversial Talk Radio	Does exactly what it says on the tin
Heart-Rant FM	Nice controversial radio
Five Live	Sport and news radio
Five Alive	Not actually a radio station but a brand of fruit juice
Five Live Gold	Memorable phone-ins and old topical discussions
Radio Active	News from the nuclear industry
Radio Passive	Soothing music for the ill and infirm of the Sellafield area
Salsa FM	24-hour salsa music
Latin FM	Gerundives and irregular verbs around the clock
Terry's All Gold hits	Terry Wogan plays a selection of million-selling hits
London Guatemala Radio	News and views for the London Guatemalan community
Radio Therapy	24-hour agony advice
Melody FM	24-hour agony
Radio Free Europe	American propaganda station
Radio Free London	Classical music for Cockneys
Radio Ham	Broadcasting to small Surrey suburb of Ham
Radio W.O.L.D.D.D.	Morning-only radio
Radio Stow-on-the-W.O.L.D.D.D.	Morning-only radio for the Gloucestershire area
Radio LNER	Trainspotters' radio

Wedding lists of the stars

The Wedding List of

Mr Elton John
and Mr David Furnish

Matching 'his' and 'his' towels
Rug (floor)
Rug (head)
Matching rings
Arab strap
Arab
Judy Garland box set
Centre-forward
(for transfer to Watford FC after
2 weeks home trial)
Lager flavoured knacker drops
Louis Quatorze fisting plinth

The Wedding List of
Mr David Beckham and
Ms Victoria 'Posh Spice' Adam

Plastic flying ducks
The entire Lilliput Lane miniatures set
Framed crying child poster
Woolworths pick 'n' mix voucher
White leather L-shaped sofa with built-in love
Welsh-lady-in-traditional-dress lavatory roll co
Books (3ft x 4ft, spines only,
to conceal Dallas videotapes)
Case of Asti Spumante for laying down
Table nest for living room
Machine-gun nest for outer gate
Mahogany-effect TV remote control
Lager flavoured knacker drops
Pint of whelks

WEDDING LIST OF
MR LIAM GALLAGHER AND
MS. PATSY KENSIT

Colombian confetti
3- tiered wedding coke
Breville coke toaster
Beatles song book
Divorce lawyer
Bert Weedon play-in-a-day-book
Shakermaker
Cigarettes
Alcohol
Silver- plated eyebrow tweezers
Manchester City Football Club

Cook Towers
                              Brighton
                              Nowhere near Hull

From: Fatboy Slim
To: Bri-Bri-Bri-Bri-Bri-Bri-Bri British Gas

Date: Right About Now

Dear Dear Dear Dear Dear Dear Dear Dear Dear Dear Dear
Dear Dear Dear Dear Dear Sir

I shooooooooooooooooooooooooooooooould like you to
check my faulty gas meter. My faulty gas meter check
it out now, out now, out now, out- out- out- out- out-
out-ouuuuuuuuuuuuuuuu. Check it out now, get a funk
soul brother to check it out now. A funk soul brother,
check it out now. A funk soul brother, check it out
out out out out out out   ..Right about now. Can he
come and check my meter right about now? My faulty gas
meter right about now. My faulty gas meter right abou-
bou-bou-bou-bou-bou-bou-bout now.

Yoooooooooooours fai - fai - fai - fai - faithfully

[signature]   *JATBOY SLIM*

PPPPPPPPPPPPPPPPPPPPPPPS

Dear Dear Dear Dear Dear Dear Dear Dear Dear Dear Dear
Dear Dear Dear Dear Dear Dear Dear Dear Sir

Check it out now. My faulty gas meter check it out now
out now out now out now out now out now out now out now
out now out now out now out now out now out now out now
out now out now out now out now out now out now out now
out now out now out now out now out now out now out now
out now out now out now out now out now out now out now
out now out now out now out now out now out now out now
out now out now out now out now out now out now out now
out now out now out now out now out now out now out now
out now out now out now out now out now out now out now
out now out now out now out now out now out now out now
out now out now out now out now out now out now out now
out now out now out now out now out now out now out now
out now out now out now out now out now out now out now
out now out now out now out now out now out now out now
out now out now out now out now out now out now out now
out now out now out now out now out now out now out now
out now out now out now out now out now out now out now
out now out now out now out now out now out now out now
out now out now out now out now out now

IDENTITY

PILOT

Winsome Scots chaps, **PILOT**, took off with the supersonic number one 'January' in 1975. There are five to choose from here, but which is the **PILOT** – and which are just cabin staff?
Is it...

Number one, Swiss Air?
Number two, Virgin Air?
Number three, Thin Air?
Number four, Thick Air?
Or number five, Aer Lingus?

NODDY HOLDER
Nobody ever knows the drummers in bands anyway.

BOY GEORGE
I do. Intimately.

SEAN Would you just take off your trousers for George, please?

BOY GEORGE
I think number one likes you.

SEAN Then I don't like him. It has to be a mutual thing in this day and age. Two's kind of cute, though.

NODDY HOLDER
Three looks very nonchalant, doesn't he? He's sort of not looking at us, isn't he?

SEAN Nah. You wouldn't look nonchalant if you were the drummer in Pilot, would you?

BOY GEORGE
It's number four. He's looking ahead and everyone else is looking away.

SEAN Oh, yeah, right. That'll be it, then. I reckon it's five.

NODDY HOLDER
Yeah, five looks embarrassed.

MARK Would the real Stuart Tosh of Pilot please step forward?

PARADE

CONNECTIONS

IGGY POP AND PINK FLOYD

Can you find the link between that white-hot livewire, the taut-torsoed wild man of rock Mr Iggy Pop, and those ponderous old stately home-owners Pink Floyd?

PHILL Blimey! That Carol Smillie's let herself go a bit, hasn't she?

TONY WRIGHT Iggy Pop and Pink Floyd. I know – they're both alcopops.

PHILL The Floyd once sang about 'The Wall' – 'walls' being the imagery – and Iggy Pop used to drive an ice-cream van?

TONY WRIGHT 'Lust for Life' is actually the name of a film about Vincent van Gogh, the artist …

MARK That's right.

TONY WRIGHT …and Pink Floyd make you want to chop your ears off.

MARK I'll give you a point for that because I very much enjoyed it.

JEFF GREEN It's a fix.

PHILL No, Jeff, it is not.

MARK You're not supposed to say that yet, fatty.

PHILL Easy, grease boy.

ANSWER:

The bizarre connection is that both have won honours from America's National Association of Brick Distributors. Iggy received his prestigious trophy for services to the brick industry following the release of his 'Brick by Brick' album, while the Floyd got theirs for the video to their 1979 number one, 'Another Brick in the Wall'. When Iggy received his award, his words of acceptance were: 'If we had more bricks, there'd probably be world peace by now ...'

In July 1990, Pink Floyd's Roger Waters performed 'The Wall' in front of 200,000 fans in West Berlin. During the concert, seventeen people were shot trying to escape into East Germany.

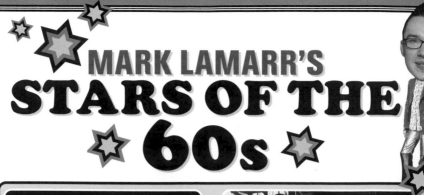

MARK LAMARR'S STARS OF THE 60s

THE MAMAS AND THE PAPAS

In July 1974, Mama Cass died while staying in a London flat after choking on a sandwich. Strangely, Keith Moon of The Who died in the same flat a few years later. He tripped over her body and banged his head on the sink.

BILLY J KRAMER

Billy Kramer added the J on the advice of John Lennon, in order to distinguish himself from other singers called Billy. It was an idea also briefly tried by Engelbert J Humperdinck, LL J Cool J, and JJ J Cale.

BEN E KING

After years without a hit, Ben E. King shot to number one with 'Stand By Me', when it was used in a Levi's commercial. A desperate search through his back catalogue led to the follow-up, the haunting soul ballad 'I Feel Like Chicken Tonight'.

THE ROLLING STONES

The Stones' Keith Richards is rumoured to travel to Switzerland twice a year to have his blood changed. The new blood is fresh and toxin free, while the old blood has a street value of a hundred thousand dollars.

FRANK SINATRA

All his life, Frank Sinatra was plagued by allegations of links with the Mafia; rumours which only came about because of his lifelong links with the Mafia.

MARVIN GAYE

In the late 1970s Marvin Gaye released an album, the profits of which went towards paying his divorce settlement. So expect about ten Rolling Stones albums before Christmas.

WORD UP

THE HISTORY OF POP LYRIC WRITING HAS GIVEN US A GLOSSARY OF BIZARRE NEW WORDS AND PHRASES. 'WORD UP' IS ABOUT THE MEANINGS OF OBSCURE LYRICS EVERYWHERE.

'COLITAS' from HOTEL CALIFORNIA by THE EAGLES

Dreary American country rockers the Eagles had one of their biggest hits in 1977 with *'HOTEL CALIFORNIA'*. However, one verse incorporates a particularly odd word.

The verse describes a night journey through the desert, during which the smell of *'COLITAS'* wafts through the air.

So who, what, why, where or how is *'COLITAS'*?

SEAN The singer's a drug fiend – he's just making up words. The rest of them are going: 'What the hell's he on about? Let's do a big solo.'

MARK OWEN I don't really remember the Eagles. Apparently, they were a massive five-piece who all went solo and flopped. Hmm … that sounds familiar.

SEAN They couldn't dance. You're much better than they are, Mark.

MARK OWEN I think he's actually saying: 'The warm smell of Colette's arse'.

RICHARD MORTON Is it the American pronunciation of 'colitis' – a very nasty bowel disease? They all have colostomies and are going to cover 'Papa's Got a Brand New Bag' next.

MARK With the warm smell of Colette's arse on the b-side?

MARK OWEN Maybe it's 'Coal Eaters', which are similar to 'Odour Eaters'. It's a small pad you put in your sock, which warms you up.

SEAN It's some sort of plant.

I FOUGHT

THE ROUND THAT EXAMINES SOME OF THE BIZARRE

ROD STEWART

In November 1990, oh-so-sexy failed footballer Rod Stewart was sued by an American woman for contributing to the break-up of her fourteen-year marriage. Why? Was it because …

a) Rod had sacked her drummer husband, making him depressed and impotent?

b) Rod had wrecked her sex life by punting a ball into the audience at a gig and injuring her hand?

c) She alleged Rod had made her pregnant after he'd indulged in foreplay in a jacuzzi she later used?

RICHARD FAIRBRASS
The only person who would become impotent after sacking his drummer would be Boy George.

SEAN
The drummer was sacked, ruining his girlfriend's sex life? Maybe they should just get a drum machine and give her a vibrator. How does injuring an index finger ruin her sex life?

MARK
Oh – you know.

SEAN
Well, I really don't go to many gigs …

RICHARD FAIRBRASS
It's possible to get impregnated in a jacuzzi because the warm water would keep the spermatozoa fresh.

LEMMY
What about Florida?

RICHARD FAIRBRASS
Eh?

LEMMY
Florida. The water's warm there. The entire coast.

MARK
So, what, every woman who gets pregnant in Florida claims it was Rod Stewart having a toss off?

LEMMY
Just don't go swimming in Florida, okay?

THE LAW

LAWSUITS BROUGHT IN THE NAME OF ROCK 'N' ROLL.

RICHARD FAIRBRASS
No, it's safe in Florida because you've got the Gulf Stream, you see.

MARK
But the Gulf Stream brings it to Weymouth.

MANI
It's the West Country that's particularly fertile for women bathers.

RICHARD FAIRBRASS
That's why you never see men in the pool at the same time as synchronised swimmers. And that's why they have those nose-clips. It's theoretically possible to impregnate several women at one time in a jacuzzi.

SEAN
Well, then I'd better ring up my local gym and apologise.

MANI
Football, you know – there's a big link there, being a Scotsman and all that. Mind you, he kicked it into the crowd and broke someone's finger? I can't wear that. If he played for Scotland he'd have put it out of the ground, wouldn't he?

SEAN
We think it's the football, though.

MANI
Because Rod dribbles before he shoots.

ANSWER:
In June 1990, Patricia Boughton injured her hand at a gig at the Pine Knob Theatre in Pontiac, New Jersey. She sued Stewart because the alleged, she alleged, had made sex with her husband 'very difficult' and contributed to their break-up. Rod agreed an out-of-court settlement of $17,000.

Rod famously names his kids after his favourite songs: so far, there's Renée from 'Don't Walk Away, Renée', and Ruby from 'Ruby, Don't Take Your Love to Town'. Which is bad news for his new baby, Ra-ra-rasputin.

In 1992, Rod spent £10,000 on a huge model railway set for his New York hotel room. It remains the only decent track he's laid down in the past decade.

CONNECTIONS

DAVID DUNDAS AND SPINAL TAP

Can you find what links the unlikely pairing of well-spoken seventies one-and-a-half hit wonder David Dundas of 'Jeans On' fame, and tongue-in-cheek heavy metal potentates, the love-pump-licking Spinal Tap?

LISA I'ANSON
No.

PHILL
Well, the Tap are a band who got together as a joke, and David Dundas…

LISA I'ANSON
…is a joke.

MARK
And he's here tonight!

PHILL
I wouldn't care. I'd have him in a fight – look at him. I mean, he's an idiot. 'I put on my jeans and I feel all right.' I mean, how stupid do you have to be to be cheered up by putting your trousers on? Richard?

RICHARD FAIRBRASS
I'm happier with them off, to be honest.

LISA I'ANSON
Think about it. Christopher Guest of Spinal Tap is married to Jamie Lee Curtis and has inherited a title. I think they're both posh.

ANSWER:
The connection is nobility. David Dundas is, apparently, the second son of the Marquis of Zetland, which carries the title of 'Lord', while actor Christopher Guest – who played Spinal Tap's Nigel Tufnel – is actually the Fifth Baron Haden-Guest of Saling. This privilege means that Guest can sit in at the House of Lords.

It's not easy being an aristocrat rock star – it takes three days to trash the west wing then drive the Rolls into the moat.

A Day in the Life of Robbie Williams

Tuesday ○ **2 December 2000**

1.00pm — get up early today. Go on wagon.

1.10pm — Been on wagon for whole ten minutes

1.11pm — drunk bottle of Absinthe

1.12am — Get back with Natalie Appleton By mistake

1.20pm — Get back with Nicole Appleton

1.23pm — Break up with Nicole Appleton

1.30pm — Break up with Nicole Appleton, then realise already broken up with her.

2.00pm — have 'Nicole' tattoo changed to 'Andrea'. Run out of back

2.30pm — Start feud with Oasis

2.45pm — Start feud with Blur.

5.00pm — Start feud with Bosnian Serbs.

3.05 — Send chocolates to one of Cleopatra, or was it B*Witched?

3.10pm — Send flowers to young one in Hanson,

3.15pm — Cancel flowers to Hanson on advice of manager.

3.16pm — Drunk bottle of VODKA

3.17pm — FLIRT with ZEN

3.30pm — Discover zen is not name of girl. ☹

4 to 5 — interview

5 to 6 — grammes.

6.30pm — send flowers to Jim Corr by Accident

6.45PM — send flowers to Jim Kerr by accident

7.00pm — Rung Guy Chambers to find out how I'm getting on writing the new album.

7.45PM — SAY something disparaging about Gary Barlow

8PM — buy Big Issue from Howard.

8.04pm — buy Big Issue from Jason.

8.05pm — turn on MTV.

8.15pm — Complain to MTV that video hasn't been played for at least ten minutes

8.30pm — Drink bottle of GRAND MARNIER

8.31pm — Check into Priory.

9.00pm — check out of Priory

9.05pm — Check into nunnery.

10.00pm — Awards ceremony

10.05 — 1.00AM CAN't remember

1.00 — 2.30am — No, can't remember

2.30 — 4.00am — Not a clue.

4.30AM — BAILed. keep next Wednesday free. 😊

December

M	T	W	T	F	S	S
			1	2	3	4	5
6	7	8	9	10	11	12
13	14	15	16	17	18	19
20	21	22	23	24	25	26
27	28	29	30	31		

Ref. 11709
© 1999

MARK LAMARR'S
STARS OF THE
70s

SIOUXSIE AND THE BANSHEES
At the height of her fame, Siouxsie used to decorate herself with swastikas, something she now dismisses as just a childish phase. A defence which failed to save Hermann Goering.

THE CARPENTERS
Karen Carpenter had a lifelong battle with her weight. At one point she was so thin she used to travel to gigs by fax.

DAVID BOWIE
Bowie's most controversial album cover 'Diamond Dogs' showed him as a large dog reclining on the floor. Asked why, Bowie said it was because he wasn't allowed on the couch.

EARTH, WIND AND FIRE
The band's stage costumes were so valuable that they were forced to take out a special insurance policy: Earth, Wind, Fire and Theft.

THE STRANGLERS
Hugh Cornwell and his mates started out as the Guildford Stranglers; but after a few complaints, they decided to start a band instead.

ROXY MUSIC
The full name of Roxy Music's Brian Eno is Brian Peter George St John le Baptiste de la Salle Eno. In fact he was the first rock star to have a gatefold birth certificate.

IDENTITY

THE WURZELS

Think back, if you can, to the heatwave of 1976 – and those hot, sticky, sweaty men called *THE WURZELS*. Here are five thinly disguised country bumpkins to choose from, but oo-arr, oo-arr, oo-arr the real *WURZELS*? Could it be ...

Number one, Mark One?
Number two, Me Two?
Number three, the King of Grease?
Number four, the Wiltshire Sheep Worrier?
Or number five, Quiff Richard?

NORMAN BLAKE
 I'd like to see their hands. If they were working on a combine harvester, they'd have leathery hands.

MARK No, they were in a band.

NORMAN BLAKE
 I always thought they were real farmers.

SEAN Number one works in a post office – he's got one of those lovely faces. 'Do you want some stamps, sir?'
However, number two looks like he's seen some cider.
And number three has no idea where he is.

MATH PRIEST
 I reckon two and five.

MARK Would the real Pete Budd and Tommy Banner of The Wurzels please step forward?

PARADE

ANSWER: Numbers two and three

MARK LAMARR'S
STARS OF THE 70s

DAVID ESSEX
David Essex exploited his dark good looks by adopting a pseudo-gypsy image; although some say he took it too far during his 'Set Fire to a Fridge in a Lay-by' tour.

THE PRETENDERS
As a militant vegetarian, Pretenders star Chrissie Hynde has been urging Madonna to give up meat completely; and no doubt she will, the day they invent the Quorn cock.

ISAAC HAYES
Isaac Hayes was sent to jail in 1989. On his first day he was taken to the prison allotment and asked:
'Can you dig it?'

THE SKIDS
After leaving the Skids, frontman Richard Jobson went on to become a poet, actor, TV presenter, and even a male model during the great 'handsome model shortage' of 1982.
Skids member Stuart Adamson went on to become a Big Country member – and we all do remember.

STATUS QUO
Francis Rossi says he wrote 'Pictures of Matchstick Men' while he was sitting on the toilet at home. In fact, the original title was going to be: 'I'd give that ten minutes if I were you, love.'

TAVARES
The Tavares family consisted of five brothers: Ralph, Chubby, Butch, Pooch and Tiny. They also had a sister who couldn't sing at all – Posh Tavares.

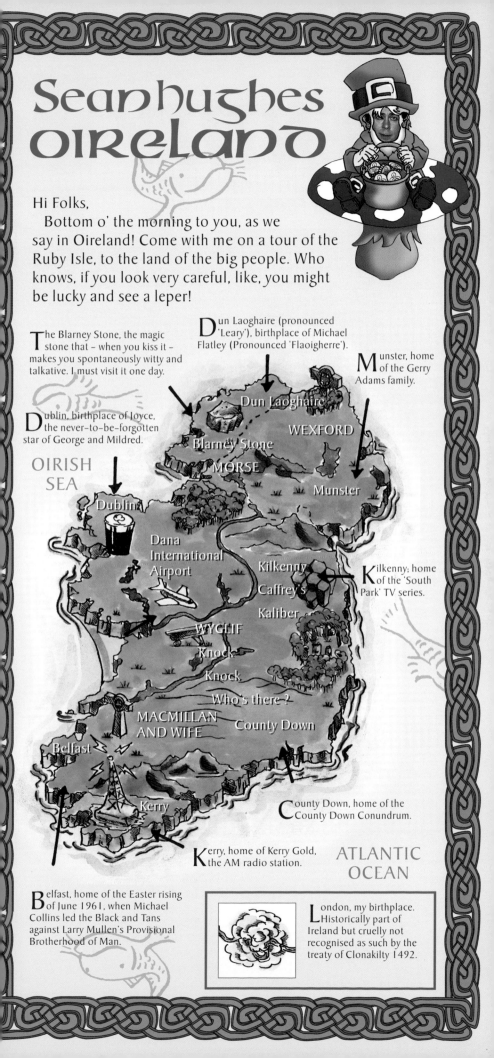

Seanhughes Oireland

Hi Folks,

   Bottom o' the morning to you, as we say in Oireland! Come with me on a tour of the Ruby Isle, to the land of the big people. Who knows, if you look very careful, like, you might be lucky and see a leper!

The Blarney Stone, the magic stone that – when you kiss it – makes you spontaneously witty and talkative. I must visit it one day.

Dun Laoghaire (pronounced 'Leary'), birthplace of Michael Flatley (Pronounced 'Flaoigherre').

Munster, home of the Gerry Adams family.

Dublin, birthplace of Joyce, the never-to-be-forgotten star of George and Mildred.

OIRISH SEA

Dun Laoghaire

WEXFORD

Blarney Stone

MORSE

Munster

Dublin

Dana International Airport

Kilkenny

Caffrey's

Kaliber

Kilkenny; home of the 'South Park' TV series.

WYCLIF

Knock

Knock

Who's there ?

MACMILLAN AND WIFE

County Down

Belfast

Kerry

County Down, home of the County Down Conundrum.

Kerry, home of Kerry Gold, the AM radio station.

ATLANTIC OCEAN

Belfast, home of the Easter rising of June 1961, when Michael Collins led the Black and Tans against Larry Mullen's Provisional Brotherhood of Man.

London, my birthplace. Historically part of Ireland but cruelly not recognised as such by the treaty of Clonakilty 1492.

IDENTITY

JOHN COGHLAN FROM STATUS QUO

Here's a man who only ever had to learn one drum pattern –
STATUS QUO'S JOHN COGHLAN. There are five boogie boys to choose
from, but only one spent seventeen years looking at Francis Rossi's
arse. Is it ...

Number one, Sweet Caroline?
Number two, Whatever You Want?
Number three, Whatever's Left?
Number four, Down Down?
Or number five, Down and Out?

PHILL I'd like to ask number two what he thought of Hoddle's
England team in the match against Chile. I'd also like to ask
number four if he's marked my geography project yet.
Number one is a stray Beach Boy – and number five looks too
much like the big fella for me to say anything.
All of these gentlemen dressed at 'Gap for Rockers'.

RICK MCMURRAY
Number three is really out of time. I bet he's a drummer.

PHILL Yeah, you'd know, drummer boy.

MARK 'Drummer boy'? What kind of an insult is that to a drummer?

PHILL It's not an insult. It's a point of reference.

MARK You can't smoke in here, Lemmy.

LEMMY I'm not smoking.

PHILL Oh well, if Lemmy's smoking then, bloody hell ...
(rolls up sleeve) can I have the gear?

LEMMY All we need now is the sex.

PHILL I believe you know the guy in question, Lemmy?

LEMMY I do, so it's a bit of a con really. I reckon it's number three.

MARK Would the real John Coghlan please reveal himself?

PARADE

CONNECTIONS

MARC BOLAN AND BING CROSBY

Can you find the link between sadly departed, pocket-sized groover and glam pixie Marc Bolan, and equally sadly departed, pipe-smoking crooner and buh-buh-boom golf-playing Mr Nice Guy Bing Crosby?

JONATHAN ROSS
I know this one. They were both the same person.

MARK Right.

JONATHAN ROSS
Now see. Marc died in a horrible car crash, didn't he?

MARK Yes …

JONATHAN ROSS
That car crash, I believe, is now the site of much remorse, and people take flowers to it. Bing died at the eighteenth hole of a golf course, I believe, which is now covered with flowers, making people really cross because they can't get the ball into the eighteenth hole.

PHILL All right. Is the link drugs? You've got Bolan there, singing about 'hub cap diamond star halos', obviously under the influence. And Bing Crosby there has the most indiscreet cocaine dealer in the world, just tipping it outside his window! 'Your gear's in here, Bing.'

JONATHAN ROSS
You're saying the pipe was crack cocaine?

LOUISE WENER

Bolan did a load of Moroccan, Bing was in 'The Road to Morocco'?

JONATHAN ROSS

Would you like me to move on to the correct answer?

MARK   Yes, please do.

JONATHAN ROSS

Because I think I know it. I remember Bowie appeared on Bing Crosby's Christmas Special singing 'Drummer Boy' – a very bizarre moment. And shortly after, Bing sadly bit the bullet, right. So Bowie came over here and he thought, 'Well, I've done one, I'll go for the double.' So he went on Marc Bolan's TV show to sing 'Heroes', and sadly Marc – uuurrrkk! No one would book Bowie on television for about seven years after that.

SEAN   Was he on the Spice Girls' Christmas Special?

JONATHAN ROSS

No, he wasn't.

SEAN   Rats!

ANSWER:
The eerie connection is that both died within weeks of recording television duets with David Bowie. In September 1977, Bowie appeared as special guest on Marc's eponymous TV show – just one week before the glam idol's untimely death in a car crash. That same month, Bowie and Bing duetted on 'Little Drummer Boy' for a US Christmas special: a week or two later, Crosby had also popped his proverbial clogs.

To commemorate the 20th anniversary of Marc Bolan's death, the council has put up a sign at the spot where he tragically died. On one side, it says: 'In Memory of a Rock 'n' Roll Legend.' On the other side, it says: 'Danger – tree.'

Bing Crosby and David Bowie may seem an unlikely pairing, but they do have one thing in common. Bing Crosby was a respected actor with a string of hit movies – and David Bowie's seen some of those films.

ROCK FAMILY TREES NUMBER 1: THE DRIFTERS

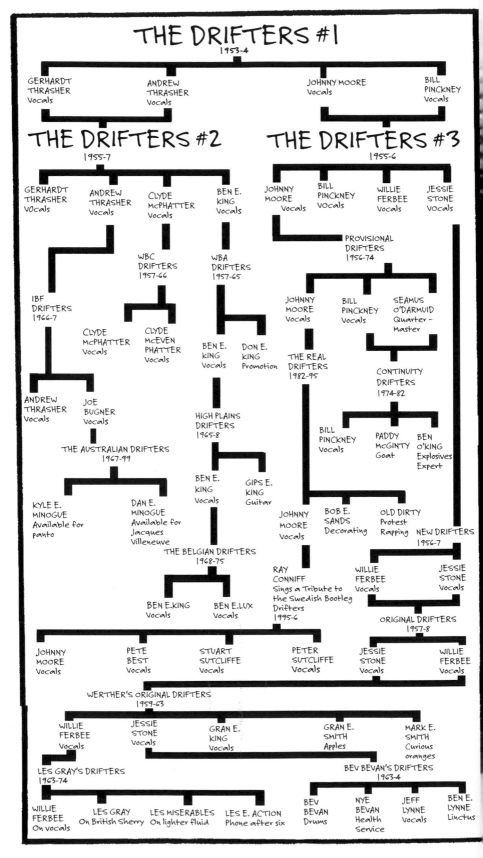

WORD UP

THE HISTORY OF POP LYRIC WRITING HAS GIVEN US A GLOSSARY OF BIZARRE NEW WORDS AND PHRASES. 'WORD UP' IS ABOUT THE MEANINGS OF OBSCURE LYRICS EVERYWHERE.

'POMPETOUS' from THE JOKER by STEVE MILLER

Despite its first being released in 1973, the Steve Miller Band had to wait seventeen years to take *'THE JOKER'* to the top of the charts. To this day, people still wonder what Steve was talking about in this line:

*'Some people call me the Space Cowboy,
Some call me the Gangster of Love,
Some people call me Maurice
Because I speak of the pompetous of love...'*

So, what do you think *'POMPETOUS'* means?

TOM ROBINSON
Isn't 'Le Pompetous' the French fire brigade?

PHILL
Yeah, but it's the 'pompetous of love' – so how does that work?

MARK
Phill, Tom's book of love is different from yours.

MATH PRIEST
I actually think it's 'Pompey-toss'. It's like the Mexican wave, but by the Portsmouth football crowd.

PHILL
Or is it the 'Pump-it-house'? You know, a knocking shop that Steve Miller used to frequent. He had code names to get in – it'd be, 'Good evening, Mr Space Cowboy. Your usual, sir?'

TOM ROBINSON
'The Space Cowboy'. He's the bloke who built the Mir Space Station, isn't he?

PHILL
'Oh yeah, I'll do you a space station, mate! Russian, are you? Oh yeah, couple of roubles – I'll get you a beauty'.

 41

I FOUGHT

THE ROUND THAT EXAMINES SOME OF THE BIZARRE

SHAUN RYDER

It comes as little surprise that toxicologist's nightmare, a rarely straight Shaun Ryder of the Happy Mondays, had a memorable case come up in a Manchester court in 1993 – but for what possible reason? Was it that ...

a) Shaun had scrawled the lyrics to 'Monkey in the Family' on his old school chemistry book?

b) Shaun left the scene of an accident he had caused by careering into a Lada driven by a vicar?

c) Shaun had told a bemused TV detector that he didn't have a licence because, and I quote, 'I never watch television, 'cos it's all bollocks.'

SEAN Monkey in the family? Is that a Manc expression for something?

JOHN MOLONEY Yes, it means that you have a family and that there might be a primate living with you.

SEAN Shaun Ryder's got children himself, right? So I'd imagine he went down to the school because his kid had said he'd been given a hundred lines. Shaun was straight down there.

JOHN MOLONEY Apparently, when he did his own exams, he got five Es. He was very happy with that.

SEAN One thing he did do was crash five cars out in Montserrat, because he was on crack cocaine. There was supposed to be a volcano there, but it was actually just Shaun Ryder, smoking away.

JOHN MOLONEY They did a drugs test on him as well. They just laid out all these drugs and Shaun knew exactly what they all were.

SEAN The TV licence sounds right because he didn't realise he had a television in his house. The guy came round and Shaun said, 'That's not a TV – that's where all the little people live.' He'd been watching the microwave for the last two years: 'I'm not paying for this, it's chicken again.'

ANSWER:
The truth is that Ryder had nipped out to buy, let's say, some 'essentials', and had crashed into the vicar's car, before driving away. He was subsequently given a ban and fined £650. But there's more to the story: when the police turned up at Shaun's house only minutes later, he claimed he'd been in all night and knew nothing about it. The police then pointed out that he'd actually left his number plate embedded in the other car.

In 1991, Shaun Ryder appeared naked in *Penthouse* – and readers really did turn straight to the classic-car article. If you'd seen the pictures, you'd know why his next band was called Black Grape.

SEAN We'll go with the TV licence.

JOHN MOLONEY I think it's the car. They said to him, 'Third party, fire and theft', and he answered, 'Well, that's a good evening out for me normally.'

THE LAW

LAWSUITS BROUGHT IN THE NAME OF ROCK 'N' ROLL.

CONNECTIONS

ZZ TOP AND JERRY LEE LEWIS

Can you find the common ground between beardy Texan boogie merchants and stadium-fillers ZZ Top, and loony-tunes Bible-thumper and hard-partying rock 'n' roll family man, Jerry Lee Lewis?

BRUCE DICKINSON

Frank Beard is ZZ Top's drummer and hasn't got a beard. And Jerry Lee Lewis hasn't got a beard, either.

BRIAN MOLKO

No, I think Jerry Lee's just discovered that his piano's less than 12 years old, so he's trying to get his leg over. Which could lead to a connection about teenage wives, possibly.

PHILL

Is it weird religions? Was Jerry Lee one of them snake-handling Southern Baptist types?

BRUCE DICKINSON

Yeah! And his cousin's Jimmy Swaggart.

PHILL

No, no. ZZ Top are Amish. They've got a stretch cart that takes them to gigs.

BRIAN MOLKO

It has something to do with bass players. The bass player from ZZ Top shot himself in the foot – and Jerry Lee Lewis shot his bass player?

ANSWER:
The connection is indeed that both acts have seen bass players involved in accidental shootings.

In September 1976, at his birthday party, Jerry Lee Lewis inadvertently pumped one into bassist Norman Owens. Some eight years later, the Top's bass man Dusty Hill stupidly shot himself in the 'lower abdomen' when the gun he carried in his cowboy boot sort of 'went off.' Although for 'abdomen' you can probably read 'bollocks.'

In 1976, ZZ Top appeared on stage with an assortment of snakes, raccoons and muskrats. It wasn't part of the show – they'd just combed their beards out that day.

There was huge controversy when Jerry Lee Lewis married his 13-year-old cousin. His family was outraged. They'd been lining him up with his younger sister.

When Jerry Lee came home and announced his marriage, his mother burst into tears and said, "So it's all over between us, then, is it?"

Paul McCartney's
Mixed Grill

SERVES I

Ingredients:

23 bacon rashers
4lbs lamb chops
4 more lbs lamb chops
lots of sausages
1 haunch venison
1 bag offal
1 bowl tripe
lard
2 doz Osprey's eggs (free range)

Method:

Smell bacon. Rethink entire life. Take 4lbs mixed vegetables and throw in bin. Take Quorn from cupboard, and jump up and down on it shouting, 'I never liked Quorn anyway!' Grill the above and serve swimming in fat. Garnish with pig's head.

Jimmy McCulloch's
❧
Three Bean Casserole

SERVES 1

Ingredients:

¼ lb Haricot beans

¼ lb Flageolet beans

¼ lb Black-eye beans

½ lb tomatoes (chopped)

2 onions (chopped)

1 pint vegetable stock

3 tsp olive oil

¼ pint wine

2 tsp oregano

1 tsp salt

1 tsp pepper

pinch of heroin

Method:

1. Chop the vegetables and simmer for thirty minutes in the stock. Don't inject the heroin at this stage.

2. After half an hour the tomatoes should have reduced, while your body will be racked with a profound heroin craving. Add the wine, oregano and seasoning. Reduce for a further ten minutes and sweat copiously.

3. Try not to shoot up at this point as you may fall into a coma, causing the pan to boil dry, thus impairing flavour.

4. When the casserole has reached the desired consistency, stir in the olive oil and serve with crusty bread, a green side salad and no heroin. Leave the heroin alone.

5. Oh, all right then, maybe just a bit. But not too much.

THE 100% MUSIC CLUB PRESENTS:

robbie williams
I've been expecting you

FREE CD WITH EVERY PURCHASE
(NOW THAT'S WHAT I CALL WASHBOARD #7)

THE MISEDUCATION OF LAURYN HILL

SEND NO MONEY NOW!
BUT SHEDLOADS LATER

MADONNA)((ray of light

oasis

5 ALBUMS FOR 99P!*

CHRISTEBY'S
A U C T I O N E E R S

325 South Clarence Street SW1

LOTS 44-51

A selection of rock memorabilia, presenting a unique investment opportunity for the serious collector, the dedicated fan or just the gullible twat.

LOT 44
Mama Cass' Sandwich Toaster
(used once)

LOT 45
Marc Bolan's false teeth
(embedded in attractive elm-bark mount)

LOT 46
Marc Almond's Pint Pot
(unusually glazed)

LOT 47
John Lennon's Bullet-proof Vest
(mint condition – i.e. with hole in middle)

. LOT 48
Geri Spice's Union Jack Knickers
(mint condition – i.e. with hole in middle)

LOT 49
Freddie Mercury's Condom
(mint condition – i.e. with hole in middle)

LOT 50
Brian Jones' Waterwings
(mint condition – i.e. with hole in middle)

LOT 51
Kurt Cobain's Head
(mint condition – i.e. with hole in middle)

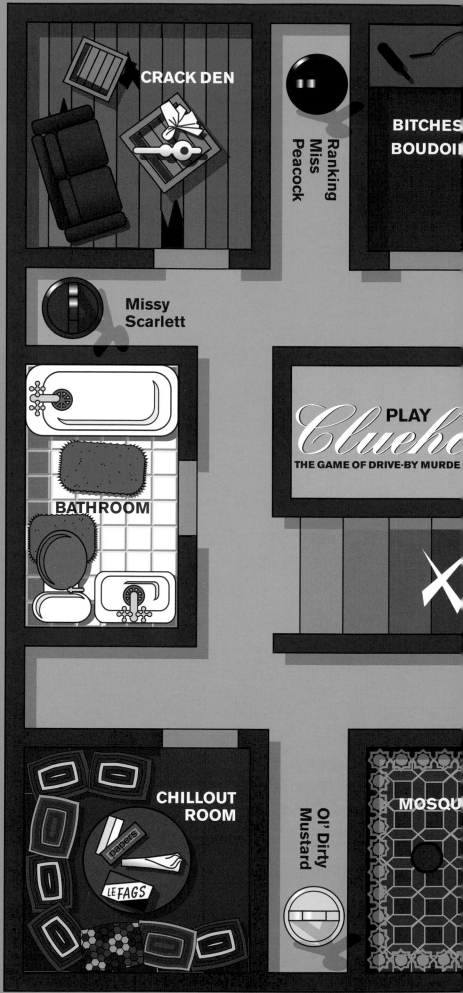

IDENTITY

EDWIN STARR

MARK   I'm sure we all recall the great *Edwin Starr* of 'War!' fame. But which of these is the real Edwin? Is it...

Number one, Six Day War?
Number two, Hundred Years War?
Number three, Evelyn Waugh?
Number four, 'What is it good for?'?
Or number five, 'Hoooooahhhh! Absolutely nothing!'

JUNIOR SIMPSON   I'm not going to take the mick too much. I could be related to one of these guys.

MARK   You mean you're black as well?

JUNIOR SIMPSON   No, it's just that I'm sure my dad used to cut some of their hair.

MARK   Number three probably wasn't a regular.

SEAN   I'm a little worried about number three. He's transfixed. He just doesn't move. Well, Edwin's just flown in from America, so who looks jetlagged? Three. They must have had a near-crash. He's traumatised.

FAYE TOZER   Well, I like number four. He's got that star quality.

SEAN   My favourite's three, obviously.

MARK   He doesn't seem so fond of you.

SEAN   Three, I love you. You're coming home with me – we're living together.

JUNIOR SIMPSON   He's the best.

SEAN   He should get time and a half. The rest have been fidgeting – he's a mannequin.

MARK   The question remains, which is Edwin Starr?

PARADE

FAYE TOZER
Number four.

MARK
Would the real Edwin Starr please make himself known? Oh, and just to set my mind at ease – would number three step forward as well? It's like the parable of the bald man that could walk.

ANSWER: Number four

53

CONNECTIONS

BJÖRK, TOYAH AND SEAN HUGHES

A three-way connection. What do you think is the link between tuneful Icelandic puffin-eating loon Björk, tuneless but lovely punk has-been Toyah and, er, tone-deaf Irish poet, Jackanory presenter and sometime comic Sean Hughes?

LOUISE I don't really know him. What's he done?

JEFF GREEN Is it three things you think of during sex when you want to delay it?

SEAN I'm so glad you're thinking about me in bed, Jeff. That's lovely.

PHILL Okay. Björk went out with Goldie, the drum and bass producer, Toyah might have had a dalliance with him earlier in her career, while Sean has had sex with Goldie, the Blue Peter dog.

SEAN Well, not full sex. It was only a blowjob, for Christ's sake …

PHILL You got into some heavy petting with her though, didn't you?

SEAN It's a she??

JEFF GREEN Is it that they've all got rare blood groups, and in an accident have to get blood off badgers?

SEAN I can't talk for the others, but that's certainly the case with me.

LOUISE There was a big thing with Björk recently when somebody posted a bomb through her door, and that.

PHILL Is it nutty, stalky fans, Mark?

ANSWER:
All three have been plagued by stalkers. In 1996 Björk was terrorised by a deranged American pest-controller, while a year or so later, Toyah received a series of disturbing messages from two obsessive German fans.

Sean, too, was recently harassed for five months with letters from an unwanted female admirer. They all said 'Dear Mr Hughes, thank you for sending us your novel. Unfortunately, we are unable ...' etc, etc.

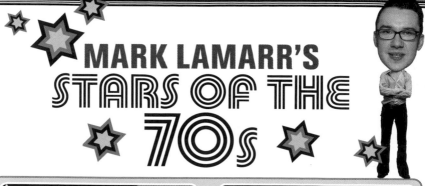

MARK LAMARR'S
STARS OF THE 70s

ROD STEWART
When Rod finally married, he pledged: 'I won't be putting my banana in anybody's fruit bowl from now on.' He didn't have time, he was too busy shagging blondes.

THE TEMPTATIONS
The Temptations' Melvin Franklin once took part in a scientific experiment to prove that his voice was so deep that he could accurately imitate an elephant's mating call. Tragically the next day he was split in half on a trip to the zoo.

THE UNDERTONES
The Undertones' biggest hit was 'My Perfect Cousin', which often replaces the Bridal March at Shetland weddings.

BONNIE TYLER
Sadly, Bonnie Tyler, the Welsh chanteuse with the distinctive gravelly face, had to cancel her annual tour this year, after she wasn't struck down with a sore throat.

ALICE COOPER
At the climax of Alice Cooper's outrageous concerts he would pay for all his terrible crimes with a bloody mock execution. Except in this country where he'd do a few hours of community service and go on safari.

THE POINTER SISTERS
During the Gulf War, the Pointer Sisters headlined a star-studded, morale-boosting concert for American troops. Saddam later blamed his defeat on the fact that he'd booked Tony Hadley out of Spandau Ballet.

WORD UP

'BOOTIE CALL' by ALL SAINTS

The next phrase to define comes from transatlantic R'n'B angels All Saints, who took *'BOOTIE CALL'* to number one in September 1998. A popular song, but do you have any idea what a *'BOOTIE CALL'* actually is?

PHILL Sunday afternoon, a lot of cars in a field, selling gear out of the back.

EMMY-KATE MONTROSE Well, we're all very aware of pregnancy in pop recently, particularly with All Saint Mel Blatt. She has needs. She has to make these needs known. She has to phone Mothercare and order baby clothes, little booties.

TOM ROBINSON No, it's something that pirates do. 'Aaaaarrhh! Jim lad, we've found the booty!'

MARK Tom Robinson and his 'pieces of eight' material, ladies and gentlemen …

PHILL It's an 0898 number for pirates. 'Looking to call a pirate? Want to talk to other pirates? Then call 0898 aaarhh!'

TOM ROBINSON Or is it a call to the Microsoft Helpline? When your computer goes down, you call it and they tell you to …

MARK Tom – try the pirate stuff again.

PHILL I think Emmy-Kate's close because a couple of Spice Girls are up the stick as well, aren't they? Posh Spice wasn't supposed to get pregnant because she was using the barrier method. But Beckham curled one round from outside the box.

EMMY-KATE MONTROSE Can I tell you what it is now? It's a phone call made to ask some one to come over and 'get it on', as it were. I know the young people's phrases of the day, thank you very much.

ANSWER!

A 'Bootie call' is jive slang for sex over the phone.

According to *The Sun*, band member Nicole Appleton can swallow a pint of Tennents in nine seconds flat. This is also a popular fantasy among fans of the Pet Shop Boys.

I FOUGHT

THE ROUND THAT EXAMINES SOME OF THE BIZARRE

WHITNEY HOUSTON

An unlikely candidate for this round is that leather-lunged, high-note-holder Whitney Houston – but, sure enough, she was the subject of a criminal action brought about by a Mr Ransom Brotherton in 1991. What was it that Dionne Warwick's favourite niece had allegedly done to this man? Was it that …

a) Whitney had punched Brotherton in the eye and threatened to have him killed?

b) Brotherton had taken great offence at her ropy rendition of 'The Star Spangled Banner' at the 25th Superbowl?

c) Whitney had got Brotherton fired from his job as a hotel receptionist after he had refused to walk her pet dog Lucy?

TOM GRAY   I think it's between the shih-tzu and the shitsong, myself. It looks like more of a muff than a dog, though, doesn't it?

PHILL   Whitney's muff? I hope she didn't take it to the Grammys with her. If the Gallagher brothers saw that, it would be straight up their noses. Imagine Liam with a dog's arse hanging out of his nose. 'Terrible gear, man!'

TOYAH WILLCOX
I heard she did take it to the Grammys and it was doing rude things to Elton John's wig. You know what little dogs do.

MARK   Good Sex Guide – she can't stop, can she?

TOYAH WILLCOX
How do you sing 'The Star Spangled Banner' badly? Was she farting it?

PHILL   We think she got the geezer sacked for not walking her dog …

THE LAW

WSUITS BROUGHT IN THE NAME OF ROCK 'N' ROLL.

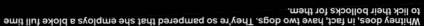

ANSWER:
Whitney Houston allegedly belted Brotherton, and issued the death threat after he'd intervened in a fight involving her brother. This time, however, the star came out on top, when Judge Lewis Paisley had the case thrown out of court on 7 May 1991.

Clean-living Whitney Houston goes to church six times a week. Mind you, so does Patsy Kensit; but that's just to get married.

Whitney does, in fact, have two dogs. They're so pampered that she employs a bloke full time to lick their bollocks for them.

CONNECTIONS

DEPECHE MODE AND MOTLEY CRÜE

Can you find the common link between inexplicably popular, tattooed lounge lizards Depeche Mode, and poodle-permed metal tosspots and Baywatch babe-magnets Motley Crüe?

PHILL   I think the connection's Essex. Depeche Mode are from Basildon, and Motley Crüe look like Essex girls.

ZÖE BALL   Which one's Tommy Lee?

PHILL   Tommy Lee's the drummer.

ZÖE BALL   The dark one? I've seen a video of him.

PHILL   Have you seen that? It's a wedding video.

ZÖE BALL   No, it's her birthday.

MARK   It would hardly be their wedding, would it? 'Here comes the bride …'

ZÖE BALL   Have you seen the bit where he honks the horn with his horn?

MARK   He honks a horn with his.

PHILL   With his penis, yes.

MARK   Right.

PHILL   And it goes 'parp parp', like that. Which is terrible, because if you were doing it with your todger you'd really want it to go 'Aaaooooooaahhh!' Wouldn't you? 'Aaaahhaah! Woop woop!'

But what it is with Mr Gahan there – Basildon's finest – and the monkey-faced, heavy-metal blond boy, is that they overdosed and died and were then brought back.

ANSWER:
The connection here is that both acts have had members who've temporarily died. On 28 May 1996, Dave Gahan's heart stopped for two whole minutes after the reckless Mode singer had injected a 'speedball' – a lethal combination of both cocaine and heroin – at the Sunset Marquee Hotel in Los Angeles. Some nine years before, Motley Crue bassist Nikki Sixx left planet Earth for a similar time after overdosing on smack at the Franklin Plaza Hotel, just up the road.
Depeche Mode's Dave Gahan was in a coma for three days, but finally woke up when he heard the monotonous bleeping of his heart monitor and thought it was his cue to sing.

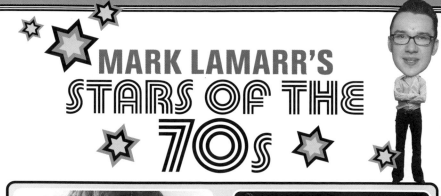

MARK LAMARR'S
STARS OF THE 70s

JOHN LENNON

Last August, the LP John Lennon was carrying when he was shot was sold for £1.8 million. The buyer returned it, because when he went to put it on the turntable he couldn't work out which hole to use.

THE WHO

At a concert in California in 1973, The Who's Keith Moon collapsed on stage after being given orange juice laced with horse tranquiliser. As he keeled over, he said, 'Hang on, this horse tranquiliser tastes a bit funny.'

THE OSMONDS

The Osmonds were members of the Mormon religion, which permits polygamy and other unusual sexual practices. So now we know what 'Puppy Love' was all about.

MUNGO JERRY

In 1971, Mungo Jerry recorded an album called 'Electronically Tested', a slogan taken from the guarantee on a condom packet. And, appropriately enough, soon afterwards the band ended in a messy split.

OZZY OSBOURNE

Following years of rock 'n' roll excess, Ozzy Osbourne now has a rigorous daily work-out. After a couple of hours, he's usually worked out what day it is.

GARY NUMAN

In December 1990, the Civil Aviation Authority licensed Gary Numan as an air display evaluator. Amazingly, there are only four in the whole country. The other three being Yazz, that girl with the hat from the Thompson Twins, and Tony Hadley out of Spandau Ballet.

INDIE BAND
NAME GENERATOR

Is your life one long round of watching the Teletubbies, forming societies you'll never attend, asking people about their A-levels, pretending to be vegetarian in order to get a shag, and taking your washing home to mum and dad? Make yourself cooler than the rest, with your knowledge of Indie bands so obscure that even they haven't heard of themselves. Simply choose pairs of names at random from the indie band name generator, one name from each column, and casually bandy them about in the college bar over a pint of 30p lager in a plastic glass. Soon you'll achieve all the alienation and unpopularity you ever dreamed of!

COLUMN 1	COLUMN 2
DISAPPOINTED	CABBAGE
SAVAGE	PENS
FOUNTAIN OF	FIREMEN
CERAMIC	KNEES
CARDBOARD	SOFAS
PALE	RADIATORS
MYSTERIOUS	TRACTORS
SONIC	PLINTH
BELGIAN	CARPETS
PERFIDIOUS	J-CLOTHS
INSIPID	GRAVY
TRANSPARENT	WOGANS
THORA HIRD'S	BALCONY

ROCK FAMILY TREES
NUMBER 2:
YES

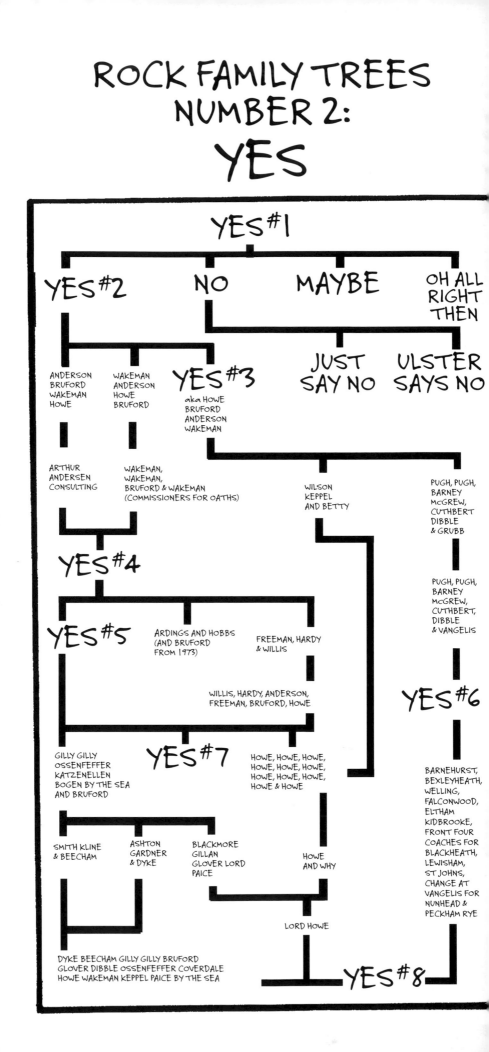

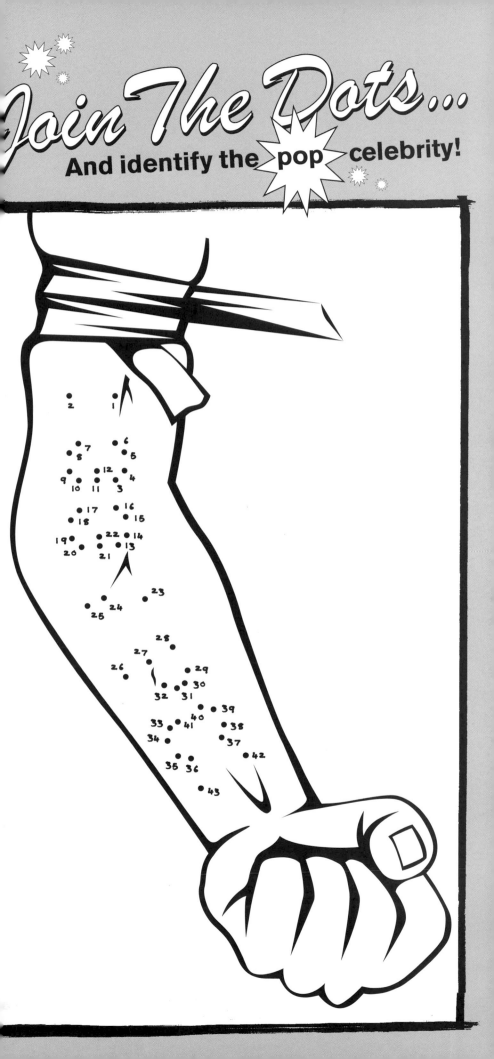

Yea, though ye walk through the valley of Rock, ye shall fear thine ignorance no longer, with Tommy Vance's...

Heavy Metal
name generator

Attention, metal muthas! Come the arockalypse, are you afeared you're going to be sacrificed as a virgin because you don't know the HM scene inside out? Are you afraid that the reason you haven't had a shag, ever, is because of your limited knowledge of HM bands? Well, it's nothing to do with that. But now you can impress your fellow Headbangers-of-Limited-Sexual-Experience with this Heavy Metal Name Generator. Simply memorise random pairs of names, one from each column, and set the controls for the heart of rock!*

Impress your friends! Hands off cock, hands on rock!

COLUMN 1	COLUMN 2
Satan's	Tendrils
Wodin's	Blood
Molten	Gonads
Waffen	Crucifix
Messiah's	Armpits
Daemon's	Harpic
Steel	Jockstrap
Vixen's	Thorax
Uranium	Nostrils
Goering's	Gusset Pump
Gandalf's	Stinkglove

NEXT LINES

When the fat one is dancing on the desk, the cross one is verbally demolishing a bemused indie-band guitarist, and the Irish one is ignoring his guests, it's easy to forget that *Never MInd the Buzzcocks* is meant to be a pop quiz. Now you too can play 'Next Lines' in the comfort of your own home and, unlike our guests, you won't be rudely interrupted. Simply shout out the line that follows each of the ones below. Answers over the page. Get all of them right and you could appear as a guest on the show!*

1   **1st**   Bad boys stick together, never sad boys

2   **1st**   Everybody needs a bosom for a pillow

3   **1st**   Crazy horses

4   **1st**   New York, London, Paris, Munich

5   **1st**   Govinda jaya jaya govinda jaya jaya

6   **1st**   Horsey, horsey, don't you stop

7   **1st**   Well she's faster than most

8   **1st**   I'm a loser baby

9   **1st**   Where do we go from here?

10 **1st**   Whatever happened to Leon Trotsky?

11 **1st**   Say hello

12 **1st**   They say that cat Shaft is a bad mother

13 **1st**   Bluetail, tailfly, Luther, in time, suntower, asking, cover, lover, june, cast, moonfast, as one changes, heart gold, leaver, soul mark, mover

14 **1st**   Hoo rah hoo rah hoo ray yay

15 **1st**   Every sha-la-la-la

16 **1st**   Young guns havin' some fun

*You will also have to have a successful pop career to achieve this.

NEXT LINES

ANSWERS

1 **2nd** Doo doo doo doo doo! Woo! Woo!
('Bad Boys' – Wham)

2 **2nd** Everybody needs a bosom
('Brimful of Asha' – Cornershop)

3 **2nd** Waaaaaaah! Waaaaaaah!
('Crazy Horses' – The Osmonds)

4 **2nd** Everybody talk about Pop Muzik
('Pop Muzik' – M)

5 **2nd** Radha ramanahari
('Govinda' – Kula Shaker)

6 **2nd** Just let your feet go clippety-clop
('Horsey Horsey' – Traditional)

7 **2nd** And she lives on the coast
('Hot Love' – T Rex)

8 **2nd** So why don't you kill me?
('Loser' – Beck)

9 **2nd** Is it down to the lake I fear?
('Love Plus One' – Haircut 100)

10 **2nd** He got an ice pick that made his ears burn
('No More Heroes' – The Stranglers)

11 **2nd** Wave goodbye
('Say Hello, Wave Goodbye' – Soft Cell)

12 **2nd** Shut your mouth!
('Shaft' – Isaac Hayes)

13 **2nd** Christian, changer, called out, saviour, moongate, climber, turn round, glider
('Siberian Khatru' – Yes)

14 **2nd** Over the hills with the swords of a thousand men
('Swords of a Thousand Men' – Tenpole Tudor)

15 **2nd** Every woah-oh-oh
('Yesterday Once More' – The Carpenters)

16 **2nd** Crazy ladies take 'em on the run
('Young Guns (Go For It)' – Wham!)

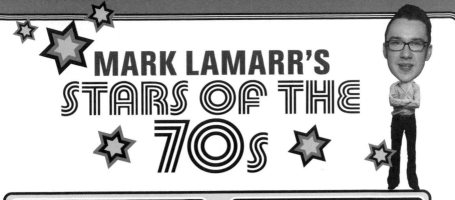

MARK LAMARR'S
STARS OF THE
70s

THE RAMONES

Earlier this year, Joey Ramone was hospitalised with severe tonsilitis, and recuperated by watching the famous Pamela Anderson and Tommy Lee sex video. 'My mouth was swollen and my throat blew up to twice its normal size,' said Pamela after the filming.

ANITA WARD

Anita Ward's 'Ring My Bell' was officially a song about telephones; but many people suspected that it was a veiled reference to sex, like Chuck Berry's 'My Ding-a-Ling', Mari Wilson's 'Telephone Man', and 'Slide It In' by Whitesnake.

LOU REED

Lou Reed's hit 'Walk On the Wild Side' was played frequently on Radio 1, even though it included a reference to 'giving head'. It was deemed innocuous by the then Chief of Censorship, David Blowjob.

STEPPENWOLF

Steppenwolf's lead singer John Kay was born virtually blind, and years of being in a heavy metal band have left him partially deaf. But on the plus side, he sure plays a mean pinball.

TOM ROBINSON

One of Tom's early hits was 'Glad To Be Gay'. Then, when he became bisexual, he released 'Having It Both Ways'. So let's hope he doesn't do a version of 'Love Me, Love My Dog'.

ALVIN STARDUST

In the early 70s, Alvin's PR people insisted that his mother answered the phone, saying, 'This is Mrs Stardust speaking, Alvin's out, do you want to speak to our Ziggy?'.

CONNECTIONS

ANDREW LLOYD WEBBER AND BILLY IDOL

Can you find the link between gorgeous, pouting composer Andrew Lloyd Webber, and bleached, transatlantic destroyer-of-motorbikes Mr Billy Idol?

ARTHUR SMITH
You say Billy Idol had a motorbike accident? Well, Andrew Lloyd Webber looks like he's had one. I know – Lloyd Webber used to write with Tim Rice, and Billy Idol likes tinned rice.

MARK
That bloke's name wasn't 'Tinned Rice'.

ARTHUR SMITH
When I met him, he was introduced to me as …

MARK
'Andrew Lloyd Webber and Tinned Rice.'

ARTHUR SMITH
… as 'This is Tinned Rice. By Ambrosia'.

MARK
Is that his wife? Ann Brosia?

JIMMY CONSTABLE
Andrew Lloyd Webber is associated with theatre, white make-up, and Billy Idol is associated with white powder?

SEAN
Jimmy! You're four years of age – what would you know about drugs?

ARTHUR SMITH
He's better looking than you are though, Sean.

MARK
Oh, that's narrowed it down, hasn't it?

ARTHUR SMITH
See, look – Billy Idol was a smackhead, and Andrew Lloyd Webber, well, you want to smack his head, don't you?

SEAN	You know the way ladies used to go for Clive Dunn? They don't any more, they go for Arthur.
MARK	Has no one ever said that you're unattractive before, Sean? You've taken this really badly, haven't you?
SEAN	Yeah, but only from Arthur, though. If Jimmy said, 'I'm better looking than you,' I'd say, 'Fair enough!' But him!
ARTHUR SMITH	I think there's some odd sexual connotation at work here. I think Lloyd Webber was married to Sarah Brightman …
SEAN	And he was the looker in that marriage. I think I can say that I'm better looking than her. Anyway, Sarah Brightman was in Hot Gossip, and I'd say Billy Idol also married someone from Hot Gossip. They both married crap dancers.

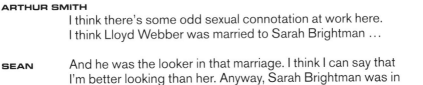

ANSWER:
The answer is that both have, at some time or other, married members of dodgy seventies dance troupe Hot Gossip. Lloyd Webber was, of course, hitched for many years to Sarah Brightman, who is better looking than Sean. Billy Idol's less-than-white wedding was with dancer Perri Lister.
In 1994 there were protests when the cover of *Rolling Stone* featured Billy Idol's arse – however, most of the protestors thought it was Andrew Lloyd Webber's face.

IDENTITY

JUNIOR

Here's the man once billed as Streatham's answer to Stevie Wonder: it's Junior Giscombe, who hit big in 1982 with 'Mama Used to Say'. But which of these five is the senior Junior, and which are just senior citizens? Is it…

Number one, Junior Choice?
Number two, Junior Disprin?
Number three, Sammy Davis Junior?
Number four, Terry & Junior?
Or number five, Number Three?

Let's stare number five out.

PHILL	'Must kill Mark. Must kill Mark.' What do you want from us? What have we done? What must we do?
SEAN	He's scaring me.
FRANK SKINNER	We'll all be really embarrassed if number five actually is Junior.
PHILL	'Mama' wouldn't have said anything – she'd have shot him at birth.
MARK	If it were number five, he'd dress up as 'mama' and live in the loft, wouldn't he?
PHILL	The bloke who advertises John Smith's bitter moves more than him, for God's sake.
LEEROY THORNHILL	So does John Lennon.
MARK	I think there's a clue in that maybe it's not number five.
PHILL	This goes to show what can happen if you take too much Viagra. 'Me whole body erect.' It's number two.
MARK	Would the real Junior step forward?

PARADE

CONNECTIONS

SUEDE AND THE MONKEES

What could the common link be between those hollow-eyed champions of the urban mini-epic Suede, and perhaps the cheekiest of those cheeky monkeys The Monkees, Mickey Dolenz of The Monkees?

BILL BAILEY

You can comb them both different ways.

MARK   Yeah?

BILL BAILEY

You can comb suede like that, and you can comb monkeys like that. Can't you?

CHRIS MOYLES

Is it that monkeys swing both ways and so does Brett Anderson?

PHILL   Davy Jones, right, was the little fellow in The Monkees. Well, 'David Jones' was actually David Bowie's original name, so The Monkees have got a bloke with David Bowie's name. Suede, of course, have a bloke with David Bowie's act.

BILL BAILEY

They both represented their country at junior javelin level. Brett's got a javelin there, just out of shot.

PHILL   Mickey Dolenz was in a series called 'Circus Boy'. Did Suede, instead of a tour van, have an amusing little car with a 'honk honk'? Perhaps not.

ANSWER:
The connection is short-lived TV robot Metal Mickey. Following the break-up of The Monkees, Dolenz became a television producer, unleashing the inspirational comedy 'Metal Mickey', which in 1982 ran for just one series – much like most ITV sitcoms. Meanwhile, Brett and the Suede boys hit the top twenty for the first time, ten years later, with the single 'Metal Mickey'.

Monkee Mike Nesmith's mother invented correcting fluid, and thus left him $47 million in her will. At least she did after he'd been at it with the Tipp-Ex.

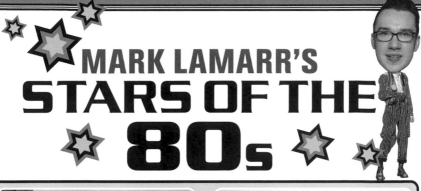

MARK LAMARR'S
STARS OF THE
80s

MARC ALMOND

Marc Almond is a big fan of Procol Harum, and once covered their 'Salty Dog'. Mind you, it wasn't salty before he covered it.

HAIRCUT 100

In one of Haircut 100's videos, the 15-year-old Patsy Kensit could be seen riding a horse. To this day, it's the most intelligent thing she's ever ridden. Haircut 100 were famous for wearing Arran sweaters, bright yellow sou'westers and lederhosen – an image based on the morning, afternoon and nightwear of Frank Bough.

HEAVEN 17

Heaven 17's Glenn Gregory used to work polishing coffins, and he also used to bone bacon. Well, after a hard day as a coffin-polisher, you have to unwind somehow.

WHAM!

These days, Wham! star Andrew Ridgeley lives in Cornwall with Keren Woodward out of Bananarama. After a ten-year search, he's finally found a partnership where he's the talented one.

THE CULT

The Cult's lead singer Ian Astbury was fasci-nated by Red Indian culture, and insisted on being known as 'Wolfchild'. By a curious coincidence, his albums were already known as 'Horseshit'. Astbury has now settled down in a country cottage, complete with big garden, friendly dog, crazy paving, and all the other members of his tribe.

THE HUMAN LEAGUE

The Human League has a history of romantic complications. One of the girls had an affair with Phil Oakey, the other one had an affair with Mike out of Buck's Fizz, while the band's Roland synthesizer was caught in bed with a Breville sandwich toaster.

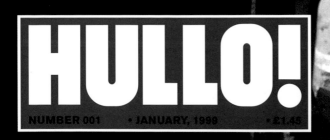

HULLO!

NUMBER 001 • JANUARY, 1999 • £1.45

SPANDAU BALLET'S

TONY HADLEY

INVITES YOU INTO HIS GLAMOROUS NEW WEST END RESIDENCE, AND SUGGESTS THAT YOU MIGHT LIKE TO CONTRIBUTE TOWARDS THE COST OF A CUP OF TEA

Former Spandau star Tony Hadley says: 'Since losing the court case I've decided to reassess my priorities. I've got rid of fripperies such as flunkies, swimming pools, money, women and happiness. Instead I'm aiming at a tauter, urban lifestyle – I'm surviving on pure instinction. My new home is very handy for the shops, especially the one I'm in the doorway of. The previous occupants were 240 packets of custard creams and there's often a lovely golden stream just outside.

The neighbours are terrific – the bloke from JoBoxers is next door, and Belouis Some lives round the corner. There's a real community spirit here – all the neighbours shout abuse at each other at all hours. In fact, I like it so much I'm thinking of acquiring the next-door box and tearing through. The pebble-dash effect, incidentally, is provided by passing office workers at chucking-out time on Friday nights.'

MR HADLEY'S WARDROBE BY SUE RYDER; HAIR BY MAD ERIC

NEXT WEEK: MIKE PETERS OUT OF THE ALARM TELLS US WHAT HE'S BEEN DOING SINCE THE HIT DRIED UP.

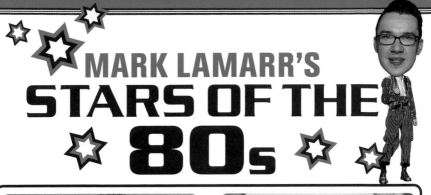

MARK LAMARR'S
STARS OF THE
80s

NIK KERSHAW
Nik Kershaw never let his famously small size interfere with his rock 'n' roll lifestyle. One especially wild night, he had a lock-in in his hotel room mini-bar.

OTTAWAN
Ottawan's first hit was D.I.S.C.O. Their follow-up was S.H.I.T.E.

KOOL AND THE GANG
In the late 80s, Kool and the Gang converted to Islam. On their next tour they were billed as 'The Soldiers of the Righteous and most Vengeful Sword of the Prophet Mohammed, in his Most Infinite Wisdom and Mercy ... and the Gang'.

SIMPLE MINDS
After Simple Minds released the seven-minute single 'Belfast Child', the IRA agreed to take part in peace talks; provided, of course, that Simple Minds decommissioned their instruments.

MARTHA AND THE MUFFINS
These days Martha and the Muffins' former bassist, Carl Finkle, is a top swimming-pool designer. Every morning he goes to the office, draws a rectangle on a piece of paper and goes home again.

JIMMY SOMERVILLE
In 1985, Jimmy Somerville was arrested and fined for gross indecency. But he hired a good accountant and got it down to net indecency.

The History of

JOHN LOGIE BAIRD WOULD BE SPINNING
IN HIS GRAVE IF HE KNEW.
HERE THEY ARE, THE GROUND-BREAKING ROCK
SHOWS THAT CHANGED
THE MUSICAL TASTES OF A NATION.
IF YOU DON'T REMEMBER THESE,
YOU WERE PROBABLY THERE.

1930s: HENRY HALL'S BANDSTAND
Featuring: George Formby, Gracie Fields, Ambrose and His Orchestra, and Geri Halliwell. The beginning of the sexual revolution. Millions of teenage girls screamed in ecstasy when Hall's hips were seen to move 1mm to the left. To avoid scandal, thereafter he was filmed only from the hairline up.

1950s: THAT'S HEP, DADDY-O!
Featuring: Billy Fury, Joe Brown, Lord Rockingham's XI and Geri Halliwell. Seminal pop show that was a must for the 11 people who owned a TV set. Saturation coverage was reached in July 1952 when all 11 tuned in – a figure that is still a dream for the producers of Channel 5's 'Pepsi Chart Show'.

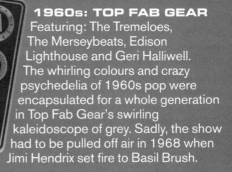

1960s: TOP FAB GEAR
Featuring: The Tremeloes, The Merseybeats, Edison Lighthouse and Geri Halliwell. The whirling colours and crazy psychedelia of 1960s pop were encapsulated for a whole generation in Top Fab Gear's swirling kaleidoscope of grey. Sadly, the show had to be pulled off air in 1968 when Jimi Hendrix set fire to Basil Brush.

Rock'N'Roll TV

1970s: THE OLD GREY BEARD TEST

Featuring: Camel, Greenslade, Hatfield and the North and Geri Halliwell. Ground-breakingly uncommercial and, indeed, unwatchable series presented by 'Snorting' Johnnie Walker. The show ran into trouble with BBC chiefs when a drum solo went on longer than the actual programme, and could still clearly be heard 20 minutes later during Panorama.

1980s: THE UNDERGROUND

Featuring: Visage, T'Pau, Blue Rondo à la Turk and Geri Halliwell. The show's pioneering hand-held camera captured the feeling of being at an actual gig and trying to pogo after 13 snakebites. It was actually a technique lifted from BBC 1's Nationwide, where it had been used inadvertently for many years. Presenter Jools Holland was eventually fired for looking into the right camera.

1990s: OH, FUCK – IT'S TFI FRIDAY

Featuring: 5ive, Alisha's Attic, The Tamperer featuring Maya, and the Spice Girls not featuring Geri Halliwell. A technological revolution in pop coverage: the show features Dolby Stereo Surround Sound, widescreen broadcasting, overhead crane shots and a revolutionary arse-mike, inserted into pop stars' rectums so they can hear what Chris Evans is saying to them.

THE MARK LAMARR STORY

THE YEAR: 1990. THE PLACE: SWINDON, IN THE HEART OF THE WEST COUNTRY. AT THE STUDIOS OF SWINDON CABLEVISION, LOCAL BOY MARK LAMARR IS HOSTING THE POPULAR FARMING QUIZ 'NEVER MIND THE BULLOCKS' ...

IDENTITY

BOB COTTON OF THE JETS

You probably remember eighties rockabilly stalwarts The Jets – but can you pick out the band's demon double-bassist, Bob Cotton? Which of these five is 100% cotton, and which are nought but artificial fibres? Is it …

Number one, Jumbo Jet?
Number two, Easy Jet?
Number three, Suffragette?
Number four, 'Jet! Whooohoohoohoo'?

Or number five, Mark Lamarr – because, let's face it, we might as well save money on an extra.

SEAN The first four are dressed up as the Fonz – but, Mark, why are you dressed up as Mr Cunningham?

MARK He's trying to scare you. Don't go for it.

SEAN We can easily scare The Jets. The Sharks were your rival gang, weren't they?

MARK That was a film, Sean. This is a band called The Jets. Please move on.

SEAN But surely that's where the name came from?

MARK No, it came from the word 'jet'. I don't want to know about your film fantasies – just choose and shut your mouth.

BILL BAILEY It's number five. It's you.

MARK Is that your final answer? Let's see if you're right, shall we? Let's see if I'm Bob Cotton of The Jets.

SEAN Fingers crossed.

MARK Would the real Bob Cotton please make himself known? Notice how still my feet are staying? Sean's team were being silly …

PARADE

87

ROCK FAMILY TREES NUMBER 3:

THE PIPES AND DRUMS AND MILITARY BAND OF THE ROYAL SCOTS DRAGOON GUARDS

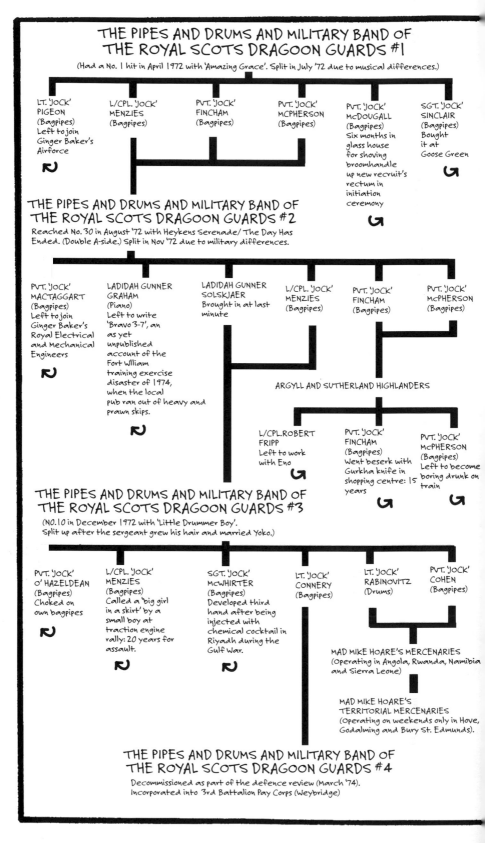

GREAT MOMENTS IN ROCK HISTORY

JOHN AND YOKO'S BED-IN FOR PEACE (1969)

ELVIS JOINS THE ARMY (1958)

DRUGS:THE

The mere mention of drugs is enough to strike fear into every parent's heart (apart from the parents who take drugs, of course). But what are the facts about drugs on the street? Is it true that the drugs don't work, as Richard Ashcroft of The Verve claimed,

Acid

EFFECTS: You begin to see things that could never happen e.g. Phill Jupitus at the salad bar saying 'No thanks, I'm full'.
Dangers: You feel strangely sympathetic to early Pink Floyd records. You're prepared to be seen dead in tie-dye.

Cocaine

EFFECTS: An intense feeling of euphoria on purchase, followed by severe depression upon realising you've paid £60 for a gramme of Harpic.
Dangers: Cocaine presents serious arsehole dangers. Take too much and you become a serious arsehole.

Heroin

EFFECTS: Small quantities give you the feeling of floating away on a cloud. Medium quantities give you the feeling of mellow, drowsy relaxation. Large quantities give you the feeling of lying in a box with six feet of earth being piled on top and a vicar being there and everything. Scary, huh?
Dangers: A tendency to develop an impenetrable Scottish accent and try to swim down the lavatory.

BRUTAL TRUTH

or are they really great as Dana suggested, when she referred to taking 'All Kinds of Everything'. Check out the pros and cons of each drug with our frank, no-holds-barred guide, before deciding which one will get you off your tits first.

Cannabis

EFFECTS: Although its effects are limited to a mild lack of inhibition, cannabis can lead the user into more serious addictions, eg Pringles or Mars Bars.

Dangers: Twenty years after taking it, people may not believe that you never inhaled.

Ecstasy

EFFECTS: You lose the ability to distinguish between music and monotonous pumping bollocks. You become indiscriminately affectionate to those around you.

Dangers: If you become too affectionate, you are liable to wake up in an S&M club, being subjected to monotonous pumping bollocks.

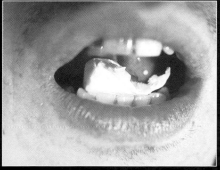

Crack

EFFECTS: Crack abuse gives you an urgent desire to rob the Post Office.

Dangers: An urgent desire on the police's part to send you to jail, where your crack will be roundly abused.

Magic Mushrooms

EFFECTS: A pleasant, satisfying experience that's almost as nice as eating real mushrooms. Best consumed with magic bacon, magic eggs and a magic fried slice.

Dangers: Being hit on the head by a golfball.

RADIO ONE

It was 1967 – the summer of love was in full swing, the Middle East was being torn asunder by the Six Day War, and it was a mere nine years before David Dundas pulled his Jeans On. But in Portland Place, just three miles from London's swinging Notting Hill, a group of broadcasting pioneers set out to realise a crazy dream. Where are they now, those ground-breaking DJs who lit the fuse for what was to become known as Wonderful Radio 1?

Kenny Everett
Now tragically dead.

Tony Blackburn
Now tragically alive.

Jimmy Young, 137
The only octogenarian in the original Radio 1 line-up. Now stands in for Mark Lamarr on Radio 2.

Dave Bonkers, 57
Now fronting the exciting 4 am slot on Bedpan FM, at the Renal Unit of Nottinghamshire General Hospital.

Chris Shed, 56
Now Christina Shed, 32, Watford housewife.

WHERE ARE THEY NOW?

Peter Dobson, 63
Creator of famous comedy characters Gervase
Hairdresser and Dr Bonkers. Now playing the
new character of a Disc Jockey who phones
radio stations looking for a job.

John Selwyn Gummer, 52
Presented the lunchtime show briefly before
disappearing without trace. To this day, no one knows
what became of him.

Sir Peter de la Billiére
Presenter of the short-lived 'Military Band
Chart Show'. Left in 1968 to pursue a
career in the army.

Johnnie Walker
Considered 'too safe' for Radio 1 in 1992,
despite the highly suspicious fact that he
could broadcast continuously for several weeks
at a time.

John Peel
Made his name championing obscure
underground acts, such as Pink Floyd,
Led Zeppelin, Genesis, Yes and
Supertramp. Luckily, by an amazing
coincidence, he went off all of them on
the same night in 1976.

Sue Hag, 69
Smokey-faced diva of the late-night airwaves.
Escaped the axe in the great clear-out of '74,
when no-one noticed she was still in the building.
Now makes the tea.

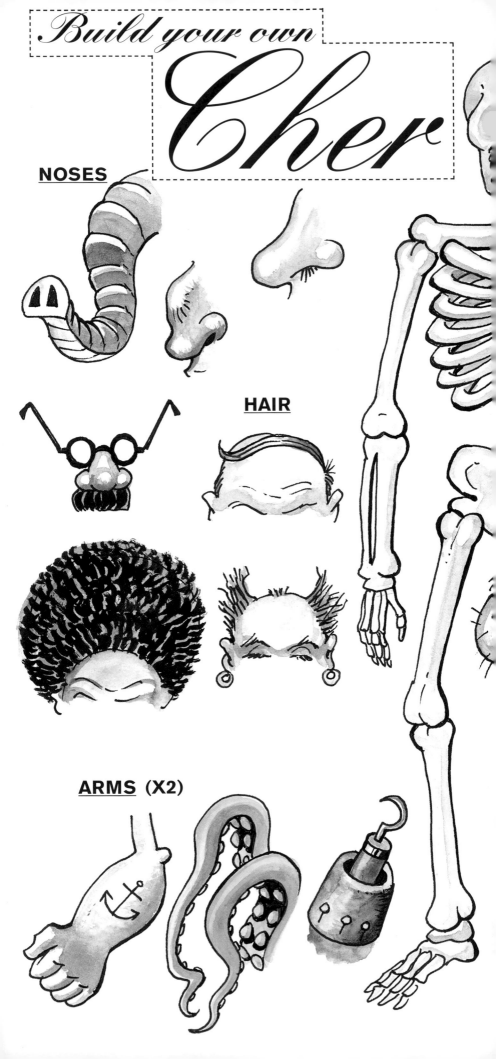

Your very own cut-out-and-keep-then-try-to-glue-back-in-because you-realise-you've-ruined-the-book Cher doll comes complete with a variety of add-on body parts. Now you too can build your own Cher, just like the real one did!

FACES

FEET

TORSO

LEGS

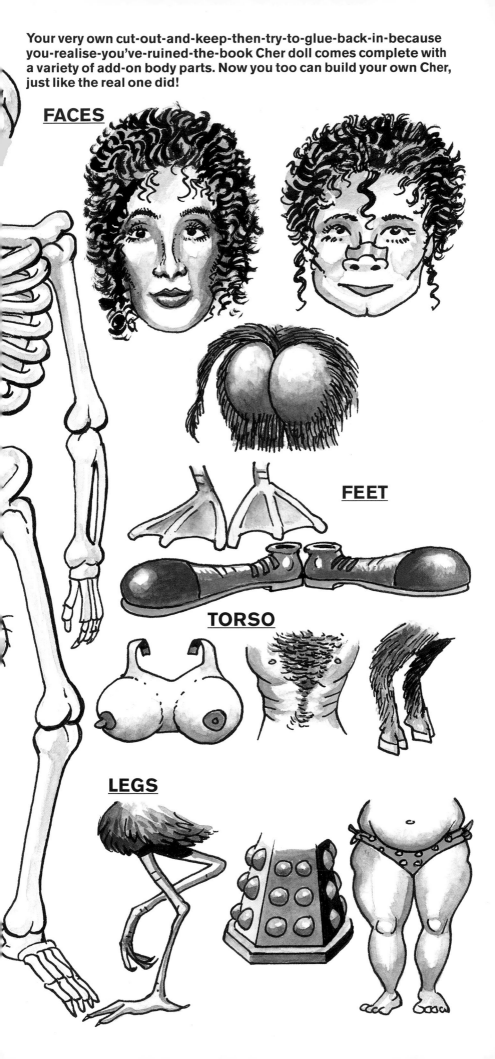

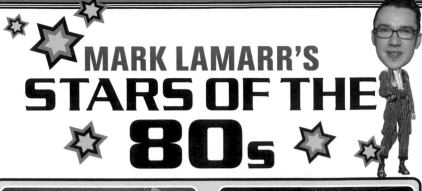

MARK LAMARR'S
STARS OF THE
80s

BRONSKI BEAT
Bronski Beat had a big following in the London gay scene of the early 80s. In fact they were the first band to receive a kneeling ovation.

BILL WYMAN
Bill Wyman's two solo hits came in the early 80s, although he was also with The Rolling Stones for 31 years through thick and thin – or Mandy Smith as she was usually known.

TIGHT FIT
Tight Fit's Denise Gyngell married producer Pete Waterman. They'd like to split up, but they're both terrified of getting half the record collection.

INXS
Police once raided the house that Michael Hutchence shared with Paula Yates, and allegedly found Marijuana, Opium, Angel Dust and Ecstasy – all playing happily together with their nanny.

THE STYLE COUNCIL
The Style Council's idea was to behave just like your local council: they had weekly meetings, believed in democratic decision-making, and had regular collections of rubbish.

FUN BOY THREE
Fun Boy Three were famous for their duets with Bananarama. Apparently they first came across Bananarama in a magazine, but then, a lot of young men did in those days.

GREAT MOMENTS IN ROCK HISTORY

SINEAD O' CONNOR RIPS UP THE POPE'S PICTURE (1992)

ABBA WIN EUROVISION SONG CONTEST (1974)

Original Drafts of the Great Lyrics

San Francisco
(Be sure to wear Flowers In Your Hair)

If you're going to ~~Newport Pagnell~~ San Francisco

Be sure to wear ~~that~~ some flowers in your hair

And if you go to ~~Newport Pagnell~~ San Francisco

You'll meet some gentle people there

~~The chances are you'll meet some other people with hats too.~~

Grandad

Grandad

Grandad

~~You smell~~ you're lovely

That's what we all think of you

~~And the police want to interview you about the incident in the swing park~~

God save the Queen

God save the Queen
the fascist regime
She's a marvellous ambassador
they made you a moron
She does a lot for the country
A potential H-bomb
And it's unfair to criticise
because she can't answer back.

Town Called Malice

Better stop dreaming of the quiet life-
Cos it's one you'll never know
And quit running for that runaway bus-
Cos their rosy days are few
And - stop apologising for the things
you've never done;
Cos time is short and life is cruel -
but it's up to us to change
This town called ~~Reading~~ Malice.

Woking Conservative Party
Woking Town Hall
Woking
WO18 7MP

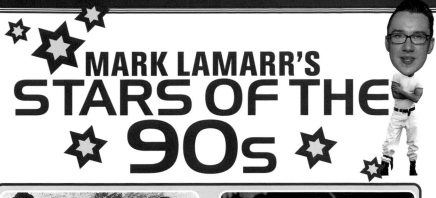

MARK LAMARR'S
STARS OF THE
90s

THE HAPPY MONDAYS
The Happy Mondays' Bez recently published his autobiography. Well, to be honest, someone else did the writing, and he sort of danced around the room a bit.

CHER
Cher recently found the long-lost wedding ring from her marriage to Sonny Bono. It turned up in her bottom drawer, in among all her bottoms.

TERRORVISION
Terrorvision's Tony Wright says his favourite things are Tequila, Scary Spice and Bradford City F.C., presumably because they all go down really easily.

THE TAMPERER
The Tamperer's big hit 'Feel It' was lifted wholesale from 'Can You Feel It', a record by Michael Jackson and his brothers. In fact the band even lifted Michael's nickname, 'The Tamperer'.

BLUR
Blur's album 'Modern Life Is Rubbish' is named after a graffiti scrawl the band saw on a wall. Which explains the title of their next album, 'Meet Me Here At 7 For Red Hot Cock Action'.

GARBAGE
Garbage's singer Shirley Manson has said: 'I loathe jokes. Hearing them fills me with disgust'. She's felt that way ever since her fat mother-in-law went to the West Indies and brought back a dog with no nose.

ROCK FAMILY TREES NUMBER 4: ELVIS COSTELLO

ELVIS COSTELLO

DECLAN McMANUS

MICK McMANUS

ELVIS COSTELLO

THE CHINESE ELVIS COSTELLO

THE PUNJABI ELVIS COSTELLO

DEIRDRE COSTELLO

ABBOTT & COSTELLO

THE COSTELLO SHOW

THE MOTOR SHOW

THE IDEAL HOME EXHIBITION

THE SUNDAY SHOW

BREAKFAST WITH FROST

THROUGH THE KEYHOLE

THE BRODSKY QUARTET

THE FORD QUARTET

BRODSKI BEAT

THE IMPOSTER

THE PRISONER

THE FUGITIVE

THE PERSUADERS

THE GAMBOLS

GEORGE & LYNNE

FLOOK BY TROG

THE COWARD BROTHERS

THE CHUCKLE BROTHERS

MOSS BROS.

BROS

DECLAN McMANUS

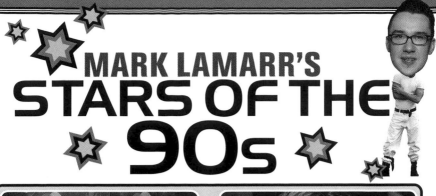

MARK LAMARR'S STARS OF THE 90s

BOYZONE
Michael Jackson was a huge fan of Boyzone – at least until he discovered it was a band, and not a backstage area.

MADONNA
Madonna's baby was born by Caesarian section. The baby apparently wanted to dodge any photographers lurking outside the normal exit.

KENICKIE
Kenickie's drummer, Johnny X, didn't actually need to earn his living in a rock band. His father, Mr X, used to win the pools every week.

THE MANIC STREET PREACHERS
During a press interview just before he disappeared, the Manics' guitarist Richey Edwards cut the words 'For Real' into his arm with a razorblade. It was just below the words: 'Milk, Mother's Pride, Toilet Duck, Plasters'.

THE CHEMICAL BROTHERS
In 1997 a music magazine described Chemical Brother Tom Rowlands as looking like Nana Mouskouri. He was so upset he started wearing contact lenses, and shaved his beard off.

THE MAVERICKS
The image-conscious lead singer of The Mavericks recently experimented with a goatee. But the neighbours heard the bleating and called the police.

THE ROLLING STONES
SURPRISE TAX BILL TOUR 1999–2004

BACKSTAGE PASS LIST TO: <u>HARVEY GOLDSMITH</u>
Please supply accreditation (laminated backstage passes) to the following:

<u>ACCESS ALL AREAS</u>

Mick Jagger
Keith Richards
Ron Wood
The other one
Mr Wood's face-ironer
Mr Richards' face-filler
Mr Jagger's stairlift operator
Mr Watts' embalmer
24 Lighting technicians
20 Sound technicians
12 Lords-a-leaping
10 Pipers piping
Rigger
Gaffer
Key Grip
Best Boy
Rostrum camera – Ken Morse
17 Dodgy Hells Angels
20 Caterers
3 Salad wranglers
5 Sushi technicians
Food taster
Food chewer

Food swallower
Marriage counsellor
Divorce technician
Crèche attendant
35 Illegitimate children
Arse-licker (C. Evans)
Wine waiter
Butler
Ostler
Chandler
Joey
Monica
Man to tell Mick the cricket scores
Honky Tonk women (6 doz. assorte
Oceanographer
Archaeologist
Opposition spokesmen on Overse
    Development
Matt from Dodgy
Meg Matthews
That bloke from *Lock, Stock and*
    Two Smoking Barrels

<u>ACCESS NO AREAS</u>

Bill Wyman

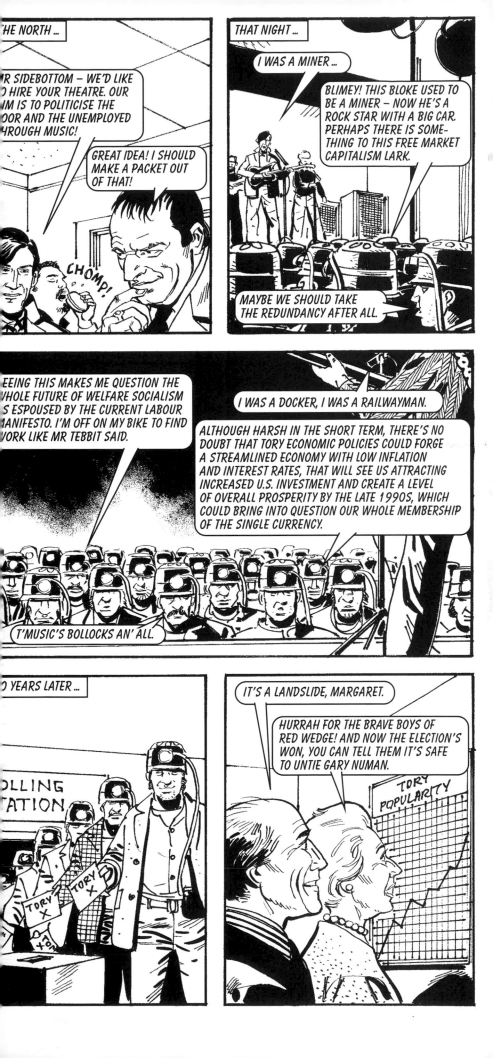

Are you fed up with being dissed by your homies? Say goodbye to Rap name inadequacy with Tim Westwood's

RAP

NAME GENERATOR

YO! I WISH I WAS BLACK!

Next time you're chillin' with your posse or just hangin' in the hood, stay ahead of the crew by memorizing some of the rap stars' names produced by the Generator below. Simply select one entry from each column at random to create your very own hip-hop star. Before long your apparently amazing Rap knowledge will be the talk of your ghetto. Amaze your ho!

COLUMN 1	COLUMN 2	COLUMN 3
Inspector	Horny	Bastard
Dr	Dirty	Mother-fucker
Chief	Sulky	Monk
MC	Dangerous	Pants
QC	A bit gross	Odd job man
Grandmaster	Really quite angry	Wheelybin
Notorious	Severely fucked off	Sheep-worrier
Flight Lieutenant	Fat	Dogbreath
Special Constable	Sad	Sandwich toaster
Admiral of the Fleet	Duplicitous	Butt sniffer
Paymaster-General	Cross-eyed	Assfondler

MARK LAMARR'S STARS OF THE 90s

VIC REEVES AND THE WONDERSTUFF
Vic Reeves is not the only comedian to join forces with a band to achieve chart success. Baddiel and Skinner have appeared with the Lightning Seeds, Keith Allen has appeared with New Order, and Charlie Drake is still fronting Simply Red.

SEAL
Seal used to put up prostitutes' cards in phone boxes. But he gave up after complaints from members of the public that he was stopping them from using the box for its proper purpose – pissing in.

GEORGE MICHAEL
Recently George Michael went out to dinner with two of the Spice Girls, but there was a slight disagreement: they wanted to go to a fancy restaurant, but George said he'd rather spend the evening in a Little Chef.

ADAMSKI
Adamski was once in a band who frequently performed naked. Girls used to throw underwear at them, and shout: 'For God's sake, put these on will you?'

ALANIS MORISSETTE
Alanis Morissette's first album sold 28 million copies, including one to a bloke.
   After the success of that album, Alanis went to India and worked with Mother Theresa, until the lepers got fed up with her constant whining.

THE SPICE GIRLS
When Spice Girl Victoria announced she was pregnant, William Hill offered odds of 14–1 on a Valentine's Day birth, 33–1 on her becoming a granny within 20 years, and 1,000–1 on her actually being posh.

You know you've made it in rock'n'roll when you take delivery of your first swimming pool. It's the ultimate rock status symbol. Here, six rock titans show us their most prized possessions.

1. THE WURZELS
Built with the help of an EU subsidy, the Somerset rockers' pool doubles as a sheep-dip and slurry pit.

2. MICHAEL JACKSON
Michael Jackson is very safety conscious and insists on a height limit for bathers: you can't use his pool if you are over three feet tall. At all times bathers are supervised by a fully qualified lawyer.

3. BRIAN JONES
Brian's pool is now for sale, although there appears to be something clogging the filtration system.

4. STING

Sting has his own leisure and swimming complex next to his house. It is so big that an area of virgin forest the size of two football pitches had to be cleared to make way for it.

5. TONY HADLEY OUT OF SPANDAU BALLET

Tony's pool parties are legendary in the rock fraternity. Sadly they have to stop at 3 pm for the Mothers' Aqua Aerobics Class.

6. GARY NUMAN

After a hard day's futuristic rocking, Gary likes nothing better than to come home and crash!

I FOUGHT

THE ROUND THAT EXAMINES SOME OF THE BIZARRE

THE CLASH

Socially conscious punk wild boys The Clash were arrested and ordered to appear before a magistrate in their heyday – but for what reason? Was it that …

a) Drummer Topper Headon had taken such a fancy to some frilly pillowcases at a Newcastle hotel that he helped himself to eight for his own bedroom?

b) Frontman Joe Strummer had ordered some naan bread in a Birmingham curry house – and then proceeded to blow his nose on it, causing a fight to ensue?

c) Bass player Paul Simonon had held a journalist down before viciously biroing 'White Riot' on his forehead?

PHILL	Nicking pillowcases? That's not very Clash, is it?
LEMMY	Yes it is.

PHILL	So what have you nicked from hotels?
LEMMY	Most things. We nicked everything that we could carry away.

PHILL	Wardrobes, Lemmy?
LEMMY	Yeah, the lot. Chambermaids. Everything.

PHILL	I can't believe Joe Strummer blew his nose on a naan.
LEMMY	I can. I can't believe the pillowcases, though.
MARK	You said you did believe the pillowcase story. Short-term memory loss, Lemmy?
LEMMY	What was that you said?

THE LAW

LAWSUITS BROUGHT IN THE NAME OF ROCK 'N' ROLL.

PHILL   I think it's writing on the journalist's head. Maybe it was Danny Baker.

LEMMY   In the days before he adopted the Ken Dodd look.

PHILL   Yeah, Doddy started punk – the hair and everything.

MARK   What a lovely day to gob on your audience.

PHILL   What do you reckon, Rick?

RICK MCMURRAY
    I don't care.

LEMMY   Exactly. A true punk.

PHILL   We'll go with the naan bread …

ANSWER:
No-shit bad boys The Clash were charged with the theft of the pillowcases by the Seaton Burn Holly Inn in May 1977. The band lost the case, and the resulting fine was a staggering one hundred quid. The court case didn't stop their wild rock 'n' roll excess, though. Next time they stayed in a hotel, they took all the brochures and didn't visit any of the local attractions. In 1982, the hapless Topper Headon was charged with stealing a bus stop. On the downside, he received a court fine. On the upside, the number 37 now stops just outside his bathroom door.

GREAT MOMENTS IN ROCK HISTORY

THE BEATLES CROSSING ABBEY ROAD (1969)

THE SPICE GIRLS SACK THEIR MANAGER (1997)

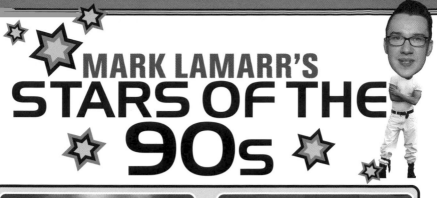

MARK LAMARR'S
STARS OF THE
90s

BRUCE SPRINGSTEEN

Bruce Springsteen wrote the music for his Oscar-winning song 'Philadelphia' before he'd seen the film. After he saw it, he was deeply shocked: 'You mean it's not about the spreadable cheese?' he asked.

OASIS

Even though Oasis have been on the road in Australia recently, Noel is continuing to write songs. So far he's written 'Waltzing Matilda', 'Two Little Boys', and the theme from 'Neighbours'.

NIRVANA

Towards the end of their career, Nirvana were really scraping the barrel. Which is probably what Kurt was doing when the gun went off.

UNDERWORLD

Underworld recently took over an ordinary semi-detached house in Romford, and converted the lounge into a state-of-the-art, hi-tech recording studio; leaving yet another heart-broken couple on 'Changing Rooms'.

2UNLIMITED

2Unlimited come from Amsterdam, where you can also buy their live videos. To avoid any embarrassment, they slip it inside a copy of 'Anal Farmyard II'.

MICHAEL JACKSON

Michael Jackson recently split from his wife Lisa Marie Presley due to irreconcilable differences. He wanted to have children and she wanted to call the authorities.

WHERE DO THEY GET

Ever wondered how your favourite chart-toppers came up with those crazy names? For instance, did YOU know that Sting, The Edge and Snoop Doggy Dogg are not what they were originally called? No? Oh, come on,

ELTON JOHN
Elton after Elton Welsby, and John after the place he met George Michael.

5IVE
Used to be known as 6ix, but one of them went solo and became 1ne.

THE POGUES
Named after Pogue Mahone, the Gaelic for 'kiss my arse', which in Shane McGowan's case is more hygienic than kissing his mouth.

SUPERTRAMP
Named after Tony Hadley out of Spandau Ballet.

VANILLA ICE
So named because he disappeared in no time and ended up on the pavement, being licked by dogs.

WET WET WET
Named after the state of Marti Pellow's sheets.

BOYZONE
Narrowly chosen ahead of Steven Gateley's suggestion – Boyzonly.

BEAUTIFUL SOUTH
After the fact that the south is beautiful, and not an ugly shithole like Hull.

BIG AUDIO DYNAMITE
The clue is in the initials.

LIVING IN A BOX
Because they could see into the future.

WE'VE GOT A FUZZBOX AND WE'RE GOING TO USE IT
Named after the original bassist Brian We'vegotafuzzboxandwe'regoingtouseit.

TORI AMOS
A mishearing of popular Tory MP David Amess.

BRYAN ADAMS
Arose from a discussion between Mr and Mrs Adams as to what their son's name should be.

CURIOSITY KILLED THE CAT
Don't know, don't want to know.

DR DRE
Originally meant to be Dr Dread Killa and the Urban Warriors of Kool, but sadly he became the victim of a drive-by shooting halfway through devising his name.

EVERYTHING BUT THE GIRL
Named after who or what Ben Watt would be prepared to shag to get into the band.

you must have known that. I mean, they don't even sound like proper names. Well, here's your chance to wise up, as we reveal the stories that lie behind the giants of pop ...

FOO FIGHTERS — Named after their readiness to fight Foo, wherever or whenever it may rear its head.

COURTNEY LOVE'S HOLE — Named after Kurt Cobain's head.

k.d. lang — Named after e.e. cummings

JAMIROQUAI — Lead singer Jason Kay, on being offered marmalade as part of his breakfast, replied, 'No, it's jam I require.' The phrase stuck.

RAY PARKER JR — Named after his mother, Camilla Parker Jr.

911 — Because their fans fit into the age range 9–11.

PJ HARVEY — Named after the singer's musical inspirations, PJ Proby and Brian Harvey out of East 17.

THE JACKSON FIVE — Named after Michael Jackson, and the average age of his 'special friends'.

JOY DIVISION — The name of the cleaning lady who found Ian Curtis.

BUCK'S FIZZ — Named after their coach driver's favourite tipple.

TALKING HEADS — Named after a series of Alan Bennett monologues starring Thora Hird.

AXL ROSE — An anagram of 'Oral Sex'.

DONNY OSMOND — An anagram of 'Mormon orgasm'.

R. KELLY — Took the 'Kelly' from his surname, Kelly, and the 'R' by ingeniously contracting his first name, Roger.

IGGY POP — Took the 'Pop' from the type of music he played, and the 'Iggy' from the way he felt after taking that many drugs.

SPANDAU BALLET — 'Spandau' came from the prison they should have been locked up in, and 'Ballet', well, because they looked like a bunch of nancies.

BJÖRK — The sound made by an Icelandic photojournalist when punched in the face at an airport.

TANITA TIKARAM — For two persons, requires 24 hours' notice.

MELODY MAKER CLASSIFIEDS

WANTED

SUEDE seek guitarist. Must have working knowledge of all David Bowie numbers 1972–4. Apply in lipstick to B. Anderson, Godalming.

PROG. ROCK BAND require guitarist. Timewasters preferred. Apply Anderson Bruford Bruford Howe Anderson.

MARILYN MANSON requires band member. No weirdos please. Box 666.

HEAVY METAL BAND requires German speaker to advise on correct use of umlauts. Apply 21 Chürch Avenüe, Pürfleet.

CORNERSHOP seeks Sikh. Apply to Cornershop (no more than 2 children at a time please).

DEF LEPPARD drummer offers wristwatch. No second hand. Will swap for Alvin Stardust's other glove. PO Box 713

MANIC STREET PREACHERS no longer seeking guitarist, owing to massive upturn in sales.

GARY BARLOW seeks time machine. Box 714.

CHER offcuts available. Prices available on application.

BIG ISSUE NOS 1–473. Complete collection. Apply T. Hadley, c/o S. Ballet, Cardboard Box no.27, Embankment.

QUORN FOR SALE. 20 crates. Apply Paul McCartney, Box 31, Sussex.

NOEL SEEKS LIAM.
Where the fuck are you? We're onstage in ten minutes!

STEVIE WONDER
seeks band. Oh, sorry, you've been here all along.

MICK JAGGER seeks AB negative blood for paternity test. Boxes 69–96.

MANAGER required 'til end of week. Apply Geri Halliwell, Box 24.

OOH TO BE AAH! The Kajagoogoo fanzine. Full set available, issues 1–2. Complete with Paul Gambaccini rumour. Box 452.

WANTED:
Kajagoogoo fanzine, complete set. Send to Paul Gambaccini, **Box 453**

SEARCHING
for the young soul rebels. I've been searching for them everywhere, I can't find them anywhere, where have you hidden them? Brrrrrrrrrr. Apply K. Rowland, **Box 275**

WANTED:
'Fantastic hits of the 70s', mint condition. Please forward to Boyzone composition department, **Box 911**

JOIN
the Teenage Fanclub fanclub. No teenagers, **Box 39**

HUMAN LEAGUE
backing singers seek new positions. Would consider working as waitresses in cocktail bar, **Box 993**

PERSONAL

SENSITIVE Nick Drake fan, n/s, seeks similar lady for pub lunches, country walks and romantic evenings. Must bang like s-house door. Box 83.

CHRISSIE HYNDE seeks rock star husband for brief marriage. No time wasters or Kinks members. Box 277.

NSM, GSOH, seeks vowel please, Carol. Box 44.

FRESH-FACED, Christian pop baronet seeks young man for regular celibacy sessions. Box 296.

BLONDE,
blue eyes, saw you at Nik Kershaw concert. You were the other person there. Apply Mrs Kershaw, Basildon.

'IRISH' poet seeks reader. Apply SH, London.

BLOKE in Corrs seeks attention. Box 95.

DAVE DEE,
Dozy, Mick and Tich seek replacement band member. Must be called Beaky. Box 143

HEADRILLAZ
'n' Da Lench Mobb seek spellchekka. Bokks 195

CHESNEY HAWKES
seeks stalker to restore flagging career, Box 351

IN THE COURTS
SPANDAU BALLET vs GARY KEMP

SENTENCES:

Tony Hadley	20 years' hard labour
John Keeble	20 years' hard labour
Steve 'Plonker' Norman	20 years' hard labour

The accused asked for 'Instinction' to be taken into consideration.

IN COURT TWO:

RUN DMC vs JASON NEVINS
(WINNERS TO PLAY BRADFORD OR SCUNTHORPE)

THE END OF THE BOOK

Well, that's it then, the end of the book.
You've been marvellous readers, even during the new, unfamiliar pages.
We know you're probably thinking that the book won't end until the back
cover like most books, but believe us when we say this really *is* it.

The end. Goodnight, thank you, we love you all!

Written by: Simon Bullivant, Bill Matthews, Jeremy Simmonds, Pete Sinclair, Bob Fraser Steele, Harry Thompson

Additional Material: Mark Burton, Warren Prentice, Jim Pullin

Production Coordinator: Victoria Bobin

This book is published to accompany the television series *Never Mind the Buzzcocks*, which was first broadcast in 1996. The series was produced by TalkBack Productions for BBC Television.

Executive Producer: Peter Fincham
Co-producer: Harry Thompson
Producer: Richard Wilson

Published by BBC Worldwide Ltd,
80 Wood Lane, London W12 0TT

First published 1999
Reprinted 1999
© TalkBack Productions 1999
The moral right of the author has been asserted.

ISBN 0 563 55141 0

Commissioning Editor: Ben Dunn
Project Editor: Sally Potter
Art Director: Lisa Pettibone
Design: 4i Limited
Picture Researcher: Miriam Hyman

Printed and bound in France by Imprimerie Pollina s.a.
Colour separations by 4i Limited
Cover printed in France by Imprimerie Pollina s.a.

CD produced by Sarak Kilgarriff
Edited by David Taylor Sound
Voice-over by Peter Dickson

BBC Worldwide would like to thank the following for providing photographs and for permission to reproduce copyright material. While every effort has been made to trace and acknowledge all copyright holders, we would like to apologize should there have been any errors or omissions.

Illustrations: Jim Eldridge (pages 82–5); Keith Page (pages 108–9, 94–5); Mike White (pages 10–11, 104–5).

Photographs: Alpha; Animal Photography; Aquarius Picture Library; Barnaby's Picture Library; ©BBC; Camera Press; Chrysalis Records Ltd; Corbis; Creation Records; Graham Coxon/Food; Hulton Getty; Katz; London Features International; Mark Borkowski PR; BBC Natural History Unit Picture Library; Pictor International; Pictorial Press; Popperfoto; Redferns Picture Library; Rex Features; Retna; Courtesy Sony Music (UK) Ltd; Warner Brothers Records.

CD: Big Game Music for I Want to be Free (Bogen/Willcox); Blue Mountain Music Ltd for New Years Day (Clayton/Evans/Hewson/Mullen); Kate Bush Music Ltd for Running Up That Hill (Bush); Dreamhouse Music (GB) for Hong Kong Garden (McKay/Morris/Severin/Sioux); EMI Music Publishing Ltd for James Bond Theme (Moby Version) (Norman); EMI United Partnership Ltd for Let's Work Together (Harrison); EMI Virgin Music Ltd for Babylon's Burning (Fox/Jennings/Owen/Ruffy); Jobete Music (UK) Ltd for Baby Love (Dozier/Holland/Holland); Magnet Music Ltd (GB) (with kind permission of Warner Chappell Ltd) for My Coo Ca Choo (Shelley); Peter Maurice Music Co Ltd for Puppet on a String (Coulter/Martin); MCA Music Ltd for Teenage Kicks (O'Neill); MCA Music Ltd and Warner Chappell Music Ltd for Runaround Sue (Di Mucci/Maresca); Polygram Music Publishing Ltd for Low Rider (Allen/Brown/Dickerson/Jordan/Miler/Oskar/Scott) and Vienna (Allen/Cann/Currie/Ure); Rondor Music (London) Ltd and Windswept Pacific Music Ltd for Novocaire for the Soul (Everett/Gordenberg); Valley Music Ltd (with kind permission of MCA Music Ltd) for Pictures of Matchstick Men (Rossi); Westminster Music Ltd for Joopotor (Bolan); Windswept Pacific Music Ltd and MCA Music Ltd for Do You Know the Way to San Jose (Bacharach); Wiija Music Ltd for Brinful of Asha (Singh); Zomba Music Publishing Ltd for Fool's Gold (Brown/Squire).

Lyrics: Complete Music Limited (pages 67–8, No More Heroes); EMI Music Publishing UK (page 9, Bohemian Rhapsody; Cyanide Breathmint Music/Funky Joe Publishing/BMG Songs. All rights reserved. Used by permission (pages 67–8, Loser. Words and Music by Beck Campbell/Carl Stephenson); Hit & Run® Music (Publ.) Ltd. (pages 67–8, Govinda) Bryan Morrison Music Limited (pages 67–8, Love Plus One); In Music/Morgan Music Company Limited (page 98, Grandad); Reproduced by permission of International Music Publications Ltd.: (pages 67–8, Say Hello, Wave Goodbye. Words and music by Marc Almond and David Ball © 1981 Metropolis Limited, Warner/Chappell Music Limited, London W6 8BS; Swords of a Thousand Men. Words and music by Eddie Tudorpole © 1981 Warner Bros Music Limited, Warner/Chappell Music Limited, London W6 8BS; page 98, God Save the Queen. Words and music by Paul Cook, Glen Matlock, Steve Jones and Johnny Rotten © 1978 Warner/Chappell Music Limited, London W6 8BS); Morrison Leahy Music Limited (pages 67–8, Bad Boys, Young Guns (go for it)); Notting Hill Music (page 98, Town Called Malice); Rondor and Warner/Chappell (pages 67–8, Theme from Shaft, Siberian Khatru, Yesterday Once More); Robin Scott/Pop Muzik/BMG Music Publishing International. All rights reserved. Used by permission (pages 67–8, Pop Muzik. Words and Music by Robin Scott); lyric extract from I Don't Like Mondays reproduced by kind permission of Sherlock Holmes Music Ltd/Promostraat BV (pages 67–8); Wiija Music Limited (pages 67–8, Brimful of Asha); Windswept Pacific Music Limited (page 41, The Joker); Melody Lauren Music (pages 67–8, Crazy Horses)

Jangle jangle! Jewellery jewellery!

Now then, now then, now then! Goodness gracious – ladies and gentlemen, guys and gals! How are you all, how is the fabric of your person? As it 'appens, guys and gals, we will ask you to cast your minds back to the tremendous, the highly successful, the one and only *Never-Mind-the-Buzzcocks*, like thissss! Uhuhuhuh!

We will play a little more of the sig tune, you see, we will talk to Dignified Don and we will light up a stogie and introduce the fine trio of gentlemen who make it all possible, you see! Stand up straight!

Here to make some more dreams come true is my friend Uncle Hughes the Sean – the very marvellous comic Irish gentleman with the oh-so-lovely and hugely selling novels. Providing a most worthy opponent – although not in the pugilistic sense, for my friends are not imbibing in the acts of violence, you see – is the one and only Young Doctor Jupitus, the erstwhile Porky of the Poetic variety, goodness gracious. Finally – now then, now then, goodness gracious – last but by no means the least, the throwback of forty years ago, keeping a bequiff-ed eye on proceedings, Mr Mark of Lamarr – may the good Lord rest his soul!

I will give you one point for the artist, two points for the title! Open brackets, close brackets! Is that not right, Uncle Ted? Clunk click every trip, you seee! Stoke Mandeville, goodness gracious! We are not 'ere, we are running the marathon with all the lovely young ladies! Uhuh! The Duchess – God bless her!!! This is the age of the traaaain! When I press this button – tea-riffic! The lovely coldness of the young flesh, you see …